D1056870

BUDDHISM

&

THE CONTEMPORARY WORLD

Change and Self-Correction

By

Nolan Pliny Jacobson

SOUTHERN ILLINOIS UNIVERSITY PRESS

Carbondale and Edwardsville

Printed in the United States of America

Edited and Designed by Curtis L. Clark

Production Supervised by John DeBacher

Library of Congress Cataloging in Publication Data

Jacobson, Nolan Pliny.
Buddhism and the contemporary world.

Bibliography: p. 167
Includes index.
1. Buddhism—Doctrines.   I. Title.
BQ4150.J32   1983   294.3'42   82–5909

AACR2
ISBN 0–8093–1052–X
ISBN 0–8093–1071–6 (pbk.)

TO CHARLES HARTSHORNE

CONTENTS

ACKNOWLEDGMENTS

I WISH TO BEGIN, as my dedication suggests, by acknowledging the influence and example of Charles Hartshorne. Hartshorne is the only major American philosopher to take the time to probe Buddhist traditions and perceive there the perspectives most likely to lead individuals of the contemporary world to become the "physicians of culture" anticipated by Friedrich Nietzsche a century ago. Hartshorne was the first among growing numbers of American scientists, logicians, philosophers of religion, and metaphysicians to recognize in the Buddhist Way the cure for the encapsulation which results from enlightened self-interest, for the circularity of linguistic and symbolic systems, and for the callous disregard of the self-enjoying claims of life in all its forms. Charles Hartshorne remains the most prolific American philosopher. His writings are sprinkled with references honoring the insights of the oldest continuity in the history of philosophy—the philosophy of Buddhism.

Every part of this book except the Introduction has been read by Charles Hartshorne and Kenneth Inada, as well as by my wife, Grace, who has sought for forty years to improve my writing.

A huge debt of gratitude is also due Curtis L. Clark, whose contributions to both the form and the content of this book go far beyond the usual duties of an editor.

The central ideas have developed slowly in discussions with Buddhist and non-Buddhist philosophers since my first acquaintance with them in graduate study under Eustace Haydon, Professor in the Religions of Mankind, and Charles Hartshorne, Professor of Philosophy. Help has been extended steadily over the years by Nyānaponika Mahāthera of Kandy, Sri Lanka, by the well-known Burmese monk, U Thittila, by U Khin Maung Win, whose assistance has already been acknowledged in my previous book on Buddhism, *Buddhism: The*

Religion of Analysis (Southern Illinois University Press), and by the staff of the International Institute for Advanced Buddhistic Studies in Kaba Aye. More recent assistance of Japanese philosophers should also be acknowledged, especially in the case of Hajime Nakamura, Keiji Nishitani, Seikai Kunii, Hideo Mineshima, Seizo Ohe, and Hiroshi Kida. None in this assemblage should be held responsible for errors and omissions.

Although no part of the book has appeared previously in its present form, some passages of chapters 2 and 3 are adapted from *Eastern Buddhist* 8, no. 2 (1975): 7–37, and 9, no. 2 (1976): 43–63. A few readers may feel in chapter 5 some similarities with *Philosophy East and West* 20, no. 2 (1970): 1–23, and 19, no. 1 (1969): 17–39; also with Seizo Ohe, ed., *Life Science and Culture* (Tokyo: Kyoritsu Shuppan, 1977), pp. 30-90; also *World Fellowship of Buddhists: Bulletin* 6, no. 5 (1969): 1–8, no. 6 (1969): 8–14, and *Visakha Puja*, (May 1968), pp. 74–80; also *Eastern Buddhist* 5, no. 2 (1972): 12–43.

Grateful acknowledgment is made for permission to use excerpts from copyrighted material, as follows:

From *Nāgārjuna's Philosophy: As Presented in the Mahā-Prajñā-pāramitā-Sāstra*, by Venkata Ramanan. Copyright 1962. Reprinted by permission of Charles E. Tuttle Co., Inc., Rutland, Vermont.

From *Nāgārjuna: A Translation of His Mūlamadhyamakakārikā with an Introductory Essay*, by Kenneth K. Inada. Copyright 1970. Reprinted by permission of Hokuseido Press, Tokyo.

From *The Central Philosophy of Buddhism*, by T. R. V. Murti. Copyright 1955, 2nd ed. 1960. Reprinted by permission of Allen & Unwin, Inc., Winchester, Massachusetts.

From *Parallel Developments: A Comparative History of Ideas*, by Hajime Nakamura. Copyright 1975. Reprinted by permission of Kodansha International/USA, Ltd., New York.

From *Creative Meditation and Multi-Dimensional Consciousness*, by Lama Anagarika Govinda. Copyright 1976. Reprinted by permission of The Theosophical Publishing House, Wheaton, Illinois.

From *Buddhist Philosophy in Theory and Practice*, by Herbert V. Guenther. Copyright 1971 by Shambhala Publications, Inc. And from *Philosophy and Psychology in the Abhidharma*, by the same author. Copyright 1976 by Shambhala Publications, Inc., Reprinted by special arrangement with Shambhala Publications, Inc., 1920 13th Street, Boulder, Colorado, 80302.

From *The Tao of Physics*, by Fritjof Capra. Copyright 1975 by Fritjof Capra. Reprinted by special arrangement with Shambhala Publications, Inc., 1920 13th St., Boulder, Colorado, 80302.

From *The Divided Self*, by R. D. Laing. Copyright 1969. And from *Knots*, by the same author. Copyright 1970. Reprinted by permission of Pantheon Books, a Division of Random House, Inc., New York.

From *The Logic of Perfection*, by Charles Hartshorne. Copyright 1962. Reprinted by permission of The Open Court Publishing Company, La Salle, Illinois.

From *Creative Synthesis and Philosophic Method*, by Charles Hartshorne. Copyright 1970. Reprinted by permission of SCM Press, Ltd., London.

From *Whitehead's Philosophy*, by Charles Hartshorne. Copyright 1972. Reprinted by permission of University of Nebraska Press, Lincoln, Nebraska. And from "Whitehead, the Anglo-American Philosopher-Scientist," *Proceedings of the American Catholic Philosophical Association* 35 (1961): 163–171, by the same author. Reprinted by permission of The American Catholic Philosophical Association, The Catholic University of America, Washington, D.C.

From vol. 1 of *Collected Papers of Charles Sanders Peirce*, edited by Charles Hartshorne and Paul Weiss. Copyright 1931. And from vol. 5, same editors. Copyright 1934, 1960. Reprinted by permission of Harvard University Press.

From the writings of Alfred North Whitehead the following:

From *Process and Reality*. Copyright 1929 by Macmillan Publishing Co., Inc.; renewed 1957 by Evelyn Whitehead. From *Science and the Modern World*. Copyright 1925 by Macmillan Publishing Co., Inc.; renewed 1953 by Evelyn Whitehead.

BUDDHISM

&

THE CONTEMPORARY WORLD

1

∽∽∽∽∽∽∽∽∽∽∽∽∽∽∽∽∽∽∽∽∽∽∽∽

Introduction

THE PRESENT DANGER to all advanced civilization is on the minds of thoughtful men and women in every nation of the contemporary world. The longer humankind spins its tender thread of life through historical time, the more imperative it becomes that we drive our roots into the process of which we and all the arts of civilization are an organic part, learning to find our identity in its self-corrective qualitative flow. The greater our power, the more it becomes of paramount importance that we embody the creativity and flexibility now required if we are to free ourselves from the one-sided self-justifying cultural cocoons which have dwarfed and warped awareness and crippled cross-cultural communication. It is doubtful if there has ever been a period as unable to free itself from the natural inertia of thought, from the compulsive drives and hungers men and women appear unable to abandon, even when transparently clear to everyone else that their life-style may wreck an entire civilization. W. H. Auden, in his "New Year Letter of 1940," did not overstate the case:

> Ubiquitous within the bond of one impoverishing sky,
> Vast spiritual disorders lie.

The most turbulent times in history have been bringing to the forefront the unacknowledged perception that volatile change has become the major adversary of desperate nations and social classes, whose powerful ruling groups must live with the possibility that even the most advanced computerized culture with its video technology can neither control nor arrest the social fragmentation and dissent. We are swept along, Gunnar Myrdal complains, "by an almost automatic process driving development forward; the effects on our societies of this force for change are beyond our perception; the course of history is largely outside our control, and we do not even perceive its direction."[1]

The most important observation about Buddhism to be made at this point is that it offers, in all probability, the only viable alternative to the overtaxed economic, political, diplomatic and military measures constantly being employed to cope with the symptoms of the underlying disorder. The more fully one enters into the Buddhist orientation, the more it becomes apparent that Buddhism has struggled relentlessly for centuries with the dynamics of personal and social disaster that now threaten the good earth.

On the economic level, Buddhism has developed ways of conquering the very frustrations from which men and women of the present world suffer. Those closest to the centers of influence and power are more enslaved than others to the established order of life; they therefore find it more difficult to see that wealth, property and prestige only serve to evacuate from one's experience those original centers of vivid quality and aesthetic richness in which men and women are vitally and memorably alive. People experience the collapse of intelligence when motivations of greed and envy dominate their lives; they lose the power of seeing things as they really are, in their roundness and wholeness.

Buddhism has confronted these self-encapsulated and self-justifying ways throughout its long tradition; the roots of suffering, it has concluded, lie in the compulsive strategies people adopt in order to manage, manipulate, exploit, and direct their lives in the world toward some preconceived, predetermined end. In answer to such attitudes, a leading Buddhist scholar, Herbert V. Guenther, writes: "Since the way I travel is said to remove all bias and blindness, its nature must not be predetermined in any way; it must find its determination in the progress along it to a point which is free from all bias."[2]

On the socio-political level, Buddhism has always suspected

1. Gunnar Myrdal, *Asian Drama*, vol. 1, pp. 702–703. Full documentation for all notes can be found in the Bibliography.
2. Herbert V. Guenther, *Buddhist Philosophy in Theory and Practice*, p. 20.

the presumptions of authority uniformly associated with large-scale social institutions.[3] It has never needed the magnifying lenses of Western anthropology to see that bureaucracies and power-structures are irrational, self-serving, amoral, and that they tend to live forever.[4] Buddhism offers fresh alternatives for living to men and women whose self-defining and self-deluding cultural cocoons are being ruptured and dismembered by explosive change. It has new options for people who can no longer find richness of life within the limits of the social womb, the cultural greenhouses whose windows are being shattered by the present faulting of the institutional crust. Little worlds could once be confined by these compulsive, narcissistic, self-isolating social stockades; families could once rear the young in the image of the ancestral order; ecclesiastical traditions could use their linguistic symbols to enthrall; a military-industrial complex could maintain a perimeter guard to conduct all interchange through official self-reinforcing channels. All this has undergone drastic change; the membrane of socially acceptable behavior is being stretched to encompass all who are now alive. A way must therefore be found to unlock men and women from habit-ridden schedules and routine; the Buddhist Way is to attack the problem at the source by bringing the incessant internal dialogue to an end through meditation.[5]

On the psychological level, Buddhism brings to the contemporary world a distinctive antidote for the stress and strain that reach into the very depths of the human organism. The cure for stress, Buddhism says, is to become more widely and vividly aware. The wider the range of sensibility, the greater the resources for dealing creatively with stress, as recent research clearly shows.[6] Twenty-five centuries before Sigmund Freud, Buddhism discovered the anxiety-producing tensions of the inner life and developed rigorous disciplines of analysis and meditation to cure the fundamental disorders of selfhood

3. W. Howard Wriggins, *Ceylon*, p. 190.
4. Edward T. Hall, *Beyond Culture*, p. 218.
5. See chapter 5, "Freedom in the Buddhist Perspective."
6. See, as but one example, Hans Selye, *Stress Without Distress*.

and civilization. Men and women botched and bungled by inner conflict, false views, and conceptual proliferation[7] will participate in any holocaust in order to protect the authoritarian structures of belief and practice that appear to hold their society together.

For reasons such as these, the leading Japanese authority on Buddhism, Hajime Nakamura, has recently commented: "The East was not so unprepared for this modern age as is sometimes supposed; all that is modern in the East today is not just Western or entirely due to the impact of Western civilization; it will be seen that, concerning China, Japan, and other Asian countries, a gradual indigenous development of modern conceptions of man and ethical values, corresponding to, yet different from, those in the modern West can be seen."[8]

One of the major Buddhist resources available to the present world is the perception, probed and clarified through centuries of rigorous philosophical discussion, that the change currently being viewed in the West as an insoluble problem and the major source of psychosomatic distress[9] is one of the ontological realities of life. Buddhism locates the suffering not in the *khaṇavāda* ("fleeting moments") of experience (for these are the "really real" elements in experience and the source of our aliveness and joy) but in the compulsiveness with which people attempt to stop the world and insist upon some kind of security and predictability in their lives. It might have been possible to anticipate in broad and general terms what might happen tomorrow during the time of Neanderthal man—but change came from unexpected directions and rendered this species extinct. The pace of historical change has now outstripped the ability of most people to keep abreast. The future is forever catching us by surprise, particularly those men and women with careers devoted to predicting the main course of events. We only know that we will live even more differ-

7. Bhikkhu Nanananda, *Concept and Reality in Early Buddhist Thought*, pp. 40, 75.
8. Hajime Nakamura, *Parallel Developments*, p. 476.
9. See Louis Harris, *The Anguish of Change*.

ently in the following year. People who are caught in such riptides of change have the choice of either learning how to tread water forever or discover the Buddhist Path.

At the very time that Plato was writing about change as the mark of the unreality in things, Buddhist philosophers were defining it as intrinsic to life and as one of the conditions of life's enrichment, indeed as one of three central perspectives: *anicca* ("change"), *anattā* ("nonself"), and *dukkha* ("suffering"). This view of change is part of Buddhism's unlimited regard for the organic unity of the world; it is the first orientation in history to suggest that ultimate reality is social, a sea of becoming from which no one may withdraw. Nothing is purely private, nothing independent of its contemporaries, and nothing endures forever; everything rises and falls, comes into being and passes away, as new possibilities are actualized in the natural transitoriness of events.

This is, in fact, the central conception of Buddhism (as I discuss more fully in chapter 3). Change occurs within the process known in Sanskrit as *pratītya-samutpāda*, in Pali as *paṭicca-samuppāda*, variously translated as "interrelational origination," "creative coorigination, "conditioned genesis," "dependent origination," or simply the "interrelatedness or social nature of reality." It is almost the direct opposite of the Aristotelian and Thomist idea, which sees "pure actuality," the exhaustive realization of all possibility and value, as the source of everything, an idea whose major logical implication would make the lives of finite creatures superfluous, capable of contributing nothing to the world. Classical Aristotelian philosophy conceived the Void as Non-Being or Nothingness, unformed matter powerless to initiate activity and appear in Being. Christian doctrine located this Nothingness absolutely outside of God, the One in whom all creativity resides.

This was the dominant pattern in Western thought which led naturally to the dualisms found throughout classical philosophy—God and the world, Creation and the Void, man and nature, mind and matter, life and death, permanence and change, fact and value, mind and body, time and eternity, subject and object, self and nonself, and other mutually independent contemporaries that sunder the unity of the world's qualitative flow (Buddhism's "stream of experience").

In the Buddhist perspective, the source of everything is no determinate actuality but a creativity infinitely productive of actualities. The world is forever issuing from this fullness of existence, sometimes called *Śūnyatā* ("the Void").

The scientific revolution of quantum theory and high energy physics has produced new discoveries that confirm the Buddhist perspective. The view that matter is fundamentally events in process constituting a field of energy, an interconnected web of physical and mental relations in which the physicist is a participant rather than an observer, is a view remarkably parallel to the central conception of Buddhism. Particle physics, according to Fritjof Capra, reconceives the world "as a system of inseparable, interacting and ever-moving components with man being an integral part of this system." Capra further writes:

> In the Eastern view, the reality underlying all phenomena is beyond all forms and is therefore often said to be formless, empty or void. But this emptiness is not to be taken as mere nothingness. It is, on the contrary, the essence of all forms and the source of all life. Buddhists express the same idea when they call the ultimate reality *Śūnyatā* and affirm that it is a living Void which gives birth to all forms in the phenomenal world. Like the quantum field, it gives birth to an infinite variety of forms which it sustains and, eventually, reabsorbs.[10]

It would be a grievous error, of course, not to perceive the Buddhist difference in this remarkable parallel between modern physics and what Capra calls "the Eastern world view." The point of Buddhism has never been to acquire an interpretation of the world; the point, as Marx said, is to change it. As Capra recognizes, the Buddha did not develop his intuitions regarding the organic unity of a dynamic world into a consistent metaphysical system, and even if he had done so, his aim was quite different. Understanding abstractions does not immediately resolve human suffering; the chief interest of

10. Fritjof Capra, *The Tao of Physics*, pp. 25, 211–212.

the Buddha was to end the pain, and this is not achieved by putting the theoretical physicist's head on top of our own. Instead of inventing a new concept of the world, the Buddha provided his fellow-creatures with an orientation with the potential to awaken the individual to the ultimate momentum, the pulsations of experience, to what Claudio Naranjo has called the "patches of intense life" in the concreteness of the passing moment.

The baseline of Buddhism is the concrete experience of that freedom which is "the life process itself," as Guenther puts it in a recent book.[11] In organic unity with reality we are free, a relation and experience which not even the most valid theoretical system or culture can confer. Buddhism encourages people to stay with the flow of their own experience and to feel in its undifferentiated, objectless, nonverbal continuum the normally veiled and covered over foundations of the world, from whose unspeakable depths each individual's habit system, and perhaps most discursive thinking, turns one away.

Thinking in the Buddhist mode leads to a more fully awakened mind; one concept is better than another if it enables the individual to penetrate more deeply and encompass a wider range of life's qualitative flow. A Buddhist does not think *about* the world, as a subject surveying a range of objects; the point is to think *in* the world, as part *of* its organic unity. Thinking exhibits in its most intense form the propensity in man for becoming self-illuminating, centered in the soft underside of the mind where intellectual precision fails. The primary function of thought is to bring more of this underground of experience into the forms of more or less deliberate behavior, enabling an individual to free experience from its distortions. Persistent experience of this kind thrusts one toward fuller and more vivid participation in the life of the world, as the Bodhisattva Ideal in Mahāyāna suggests.

The original Enlightenment of Gautama Buddha was an awakening to this freedom and richness which are the basic constituents of life at the human level. Life creates us with

11. Guenther, *Buddhist Philosophy*, p. 175.

freedom to create ourselves. Its persisting focus upon the aesthetic web of reality has enabled Buddhism from the very beginning to fight against all forms of possessiveness and exploitation. Meditation and analysis penetrate every matrix of causal conditioning in the great traffic system of artificial wants and distractions. Clarification frees, enabling men and women to see their own prejudices and unconscious compulsions for the first time.

Nothing goes further to account for Buddhism's creative encounter with the contemporary world than its invitation to people everywhere to find the momentum and meaning of their lives in experience itself. It is a perspective long submerged by the cognitive bias of Western civilization, its preoccupation with the theoretical component, the postulational system. Quality has made its conspicuous entrance upon the stage of contemporary life. The Buddhist argument begins to appear plausible: suffering results when aesthetic sensibility is evacuated from an individual's experience. People refuse to be embalmed alive. Humanity differs from other forms of life in having an insatiable appetite for adding new increments of quality in its experience. "The real world," F. S. C. Northrop has written, "is the aesthetically breath-taking colorful world and it is no longer necessary to infer non-aesthetic material and mental substances whose interaction has the effect of throwing our emotive, aesthetic selves and the other directly sensed concrete facts of experience out of nature, as unreal phantasms."[12] Immediate experience is the first principle of life. Charles Peirce has probably given it its most unforgettable formulation:

What is absolutely First must be entirely separated from all conception of or reference to anything else. The First must therefore be present and immediate, so as not to be Second to a representation. It must be fresh and new, for if old it is Second to its former state. It must be initiative, original, spontaneous and free; otherwise it is Second to a determining cause. It is also something vivid and conscious (in the radical empirical sense of feeling awareness)

12. F. S. C. Northrop, Foreward to *A Whiteheadian Aesthetic*, p. xxv.

so only it avoids being the object of some sensation. It precedes all synthesis and all differentiation; it has no unity and no parts. It cannot be articulately thought; assert it and it has already lost its characteristic innocence. Stop to think of it, and it has already flown. What the world was to Adam on the day he opened his eyes to it, before he had drawn any distinctions or had become conscious of his own existence—that is First, present, immediate, fresh, new initiative, original, spontaneous, free, vivid, conscious, and evanescent. Only remember that every description of it must be false to it.[13]

Peirce's Firstness is what Gautama Buddha meant by Nirvana. Buddhism has a special commitment to allowing life to remain where it already is—in the qualities of what Gunapala Piyasena Malalasekera calls "the fulfilled *Now*." Northrop has recently commented upon the relevance of this perspective for fostering a democratic and ecological awareness in the contemporary world. It is, he argues, "both biologically and behavioristically realistic and socially achievable for any people anywhere by freely consensual, spontaneously accepted and peaceful means to self-recondition their bodily sensitive selves to compassionate relations with both their fellow men and the speechless world's living creatures."[14]

Experience, along with rigorous disciplines for extending and vivifying its range, constitutes for Buddhism an access road leading individuals out of entrapment into a sense of belonging and participating in the world's life. Throughout human history no tradition can match the Buddhist Way in its nurture of preventive therapy. It has kept men and women from cutting themselves off from the ultimate aim of life—to awaken to the more vivid flow of quality in the passing moment. It has helped them to become more fully awake, and to center their lives in the organic unity of the world as it is uncovered through meditation and critical reflection.

Rarely does an individual reared in a culture where Buddhism has been a dominant factor ever expect a belief system to give significance and richness to life. For Buddhists every-

13. *Collected Papers of Charles Sanders Peirce*, vol. 1, par. 357.
14. F. S. C. Northrop, "Naturalistic Realism and Animate Compassion," p. 202.

where, East or West, it is the nonconceptual, nontheoretical, nonverbal apprehension of reality which confers vitality and power to experience. One theory is better than another if it leads eventually to the realization that experience must be freed from theory too, freed for its rich qualitative flow. The resulting attitude encountered in predominantly Buddhist countries is that the whole point is to celebrate forever the wonder of becoming ever more vitally alive.

The Buddhist tradition has explored and elaborated upon the power of this aesthetic ontological ground in India and China, Korea and Japan, in Sri Lanka and the nations of Southeast Asia. The indigenous cultures acquired from Buddhism a deeper awareness of, as B. G. Gokhale has it, "the sense of the beautiful whether in the mystery of the primeval forest, the contours of a gigantic rock, the sound of rain on the gently swaying leaves, the majesty of an elephant or the grace of a horse, the beauty of the person of the Buddha, and even the charm of the feminine form."[15] The evidence has been deposited beyond all possible exaggeration in the art of the T'ang Dynasty (618–906) of China, the Suiko period (592–628) of Japan, the rule of King Aśoka (c. 273–237 B.C.) in India, the Silla Dynasty (c. 450–935) of Korea, and the famous pagodas and temples of South and Southeast Asia. In all of this art, minds were freed from compulsive, ego-centered drives, from violence and aggression. Buddhist art exudes a mood reminiscent of the central feature of the Enlightenment itself—liberation from the dark compulsive craving from which few people fully awaken. The masterpieces of this literature and art lead directly to the Buddhist artist himself, who has made the thirst for richness of life incarnate in his work. In art, Alfred North Whitehead writes, "the finite consciousness of mankind is appropriating as its own the infinite fecundity of nature."[16]

The Buddhist orientation offers resources for developing that

15. B. G. Gokhale, "Aesthetic Ideas in Early Buddhism," p. 242.
16. Alfred North Whitehead, *Adventures of Ideas*, p. 351.

reconciliation of aesthetic sensibilities and scientific inquiry which has been called the critical need of the modern world.[17] Millions of mature men and women perceive that the scientific technology that rose to dominance during the first decades of the commercial and industrial revolution has no aim or purpose beyond its own self-fulfilling prophecies and fragmentary conclusions. David Mandel sees signs that "our curiosity and insatiable desire for fuller experience will not let us stay where we are."

Man has an unquenchable desire [Mandel continues] to climb higher. It is his good fortune to have the road partially marked out by the pioneers, the artists. What they make concrete in their artifacts is a reality that exists in our psyches. Great art cannot mislead us. Through it we learn qualities of matter in form, and expand our sensibilities, and find levels in our minds of which we are not aware. In great art the essential nature of what we deal with in life is clarified.[18]

Buddhism reinforces the widespread feeling that the burgeoning of wealth and power, with their infectious motivations of acquisitiveness and greed, have made men and women wealthier and more powerful at the expense of the present-centeredness and qualitative richness that confer a sense of being "really real" and vitally alive. Millions of people are discovering the Buddhist alternative to everything they have been taught. They are discovering in their own experience the self-corrective and self-enjoying properties of life itself which can never be totally suppressed by the occupants of what Plato called the human cave, properties from whose encompassing wholeness even the most fragmented and displaced person can never be cast out. They are not incapable of perceiving that inflexible concentrations of syntax enable the dominant culture worlds to survive in their present pathological form. The "Zen of Seeing" shows them the dangerous lag between so-called rational forms of understanding and the drive to-

17. Richard Lannoy, *The Speaking Tree*, pp. 79, 411.
18. David Mandel, *Changing Art Changing Man*, p. 35.

ward global interdependence which no nation or social class can prevent or control. Words, they perceive, have become for many the occasion for concealing the energizing intuitions of life. The insight has never been more forcibly put than in the following tale of Hui-neng.

After listening to the nun, Wu-chin-ts'ang, reciting the *Nirvana Sutra*, Hui-neng (d. 713) explained the Sutra's meaning, which led the nun to bring a roll of the text and ask about the meaning of certain words. "I don't know written words," the monk replied, "but if you want to know the Sutra's meaning, then just ask me." Amazed at this, the nun asked, "If you can't read the words, then how can you understand their meaning?" Hui-neng responded: "The mysterious principle of all the Buddhas has nothing to do with words." The mind understands without reliance upon forms of any kind.[19]

The most penetrating minds in history probably all support Buddhism in this linguistic caution. The shared perception might be formulated in the following way to bring to mind Plato's famous passage in *Phaedo* on some of the insights that are shared everywhere by the wisest and best of men:

Wherefore, I say, let a man be of good cheer about the transitoriness of life who, having renounced the insatiable desires of the self, and the indefinite postponement of life, has cast off the culture-bound vulgarities as working harm rather than good.

Let him be of good cheer in employing the claws of wisdom, not to increase the mind's distinctive power to hate, nor to be ridden by the drive for dominion over others, but to promote that higher tropism to the light still hidden below the rim of the world. Let him discover that the enrichment of the passing moment is the meaning and end of life.

Let logic be a method for achieving that higher mode of existence, renouncing the irrational motivation to keep artfully and

19. Philip B. Yampolsky, trans. *The Platform Sutra of the Sixth Patriarch*, p. 79. The same point has been made by Martin Heidegger in his "Letter on Humanism." If we wish to apply the words to our highest value, we must "bring the clearing of the truth of Being before thought." In another essay, "The Fundamental Question of Metaphysics," he argues that "this clearing as the truth of Being itself remains concealed from metaphysics. Man must first learn to exist in the nameless."

evasively alive. Thus adorned in life's most perfect jewels—beauty and temperance and compassion—he is ready to resume that journey through the polarities of life whose consummation comes at last in union with the silent and formless source infinitely creating the world.

2

~~~~~~

The Personal Encounter

An intensified aesthetic sensibility, now at last, will decide among the many forms presenting themselves for comparison: and the majority will be let die. In the same way, a selection among the forms and usages of the higher moralities is occurring, the end of which can be only the downfall of the inferior systems. It is an age of comparison! That is its pride—but more justly also its grief. Let us not be afraid of this grief!

Friedrich Nietzsche
Aphorism 23
Human, All Too Human

THE PRESENT ENCOUNTER of Buddhism with the contemporary world is a part of the most significant event of our time, an event without precedent in the historical development of man. Hitherto humankind has always lived in pieces, in communities small enough to exercise some of our talents and capabilities, permitting mastery to be achieved in these segments before moving on to more comprehensive versions of ourselves. We have explored with great intensity these one-sided and narrow contexts in which choice and circumstance conspired that we would live.

Buddhism's encounter with the present age comes at a time when humanity may be reaching for some broader and deeper synthesis than the encapsulated civilizations of past and present, each of which clothed itself with a mythology designed to assure all members that theirs, as Joseph Campbell writes, "is the one authorized center, under heaven, of spirituality and worth." "We know today," Campbell continues, "that those mythologies are undone—or, at least, are threatening to come undone: each complacent within its own horizon, dissolving, together with its gods, in a single emergent new order of society."[1]

Buddhism is one of humanity's most persevering efforts to keep from enveloping itself in those linguistic and symbolic systems that reduce awareness and understanding to the limits of the tribe, social class, age, race, ethnic background or nation. "Man, unlike other creatures, has a specific nature; he is a determinate individual, but he is not confined to his determinate nature; he is not bound forever to his fragmentariness. He has a thirst to regain the dynamic, organic relatedness in which the richness of life consists." So taught Nāgārjuna, in some ways the Plato of the Buddhist tradition, nearly two thousand years ago.[2]

The Buddhist orientation has played a central role in humanity's continuing discovery of its organic wholeness both as individual members and as a species, and of the thousand-and-one ways we have devised to confine our living within limits maintained for a while by only a tiny part of our potential.

Life, Buddhism affirms, is one. This is the perspective required if we are to perceive the magnitude of what is taking place. The world, before our largely unseeing eyes, is today becoming a mandala suggestive of the larger womb and nurturing matrix in which it is possible to be more fully born. Beauty is working like yeast to expand the appreciative awareness of the modern world; it is being experienced in fresh and hitherto unimagined forms whose vivifying contrasts intensify and awaken a new harmony within ourselves.

Buddhism differs from all other life orientations in offering only struggle and hard work, and rigorous disciplines of meditation, to reconstruct personal habits and social institutions in ways that permit the indefinite expansion in the qualitative enrichment of life. Its emphasis upon purification expresses

1. Joseph Campbell, *The Masks of God*, vol. 2, p. 33.
2. See K. Venkata Ramanan, *Nāgārjuna's Philosophy*, p. 38.

the persuasion, tested through many centuries, that—except for the overpowering force of our greed and our unconscious self-centered clinging with body and mind—the conduits of personal energy and joy are always open. The Buddha was the first, Lama Anagarika Govinda writes, to discover "that not the results of our human thinking, but *the method* behind it is what matters."[3]

This ontological openness has enabled Buddhists through the centuries to face the full implications of the fact that the most compelling questions facing us from one end of our lives to the other cannot be looked up in an encyclopedia, dictionary, or sacred book, and that there is no place where the meaning of life is "written down." This basic honesty has militated against pretensions, against the authoritarian personality and political order, against the emperor who has no clothes. Buddhism has been willing to rest its case with ways of increasing the range and deepening the penetration individuals can achieve in their own experience. As Claudio Naranjo has recently written: "The ultimate end of meditation is its extension to ordinary life in the form of an enduring self-awareness and depth."[4] This experiential ground, the Buddha taught, is the sole authority:

Be ye not misled by report or tradition or hearsay, be not misled by proficiency in the collections, nor by mere logic or inference, nor after considering reasons, nor after reflection on and approval of some theory, nor because it fits becoming, nor out of respect for a recluse who holds it. But, Kālāmas, when you know for yourselves: These things are censured by the intelligent, these things, when performed and undertaken, conduce to loss and sorrow—then indeed do ye reject them. But if at any time ye know of yourselves: These things are profitable, they are blameless, they are praised by the intelligent; these things, when performed and undertaken, conduce to profit and happiness—then, Kālāmas, do ye, having undertaken them, abide therein.[5]

3. Lama Anagarika Govinda, *The Psychological Attitude of Early Buddhist Philosophy*, p. 40.
4. Claudio Naranjo, *The Healing Journey*, p. 22.
5. *The Book of the Gradual Sayings (Aṅguttara-Nikāya)*, vol. 1, pp. 172–173.

Meditation is the fundamental bastion of freedom—and thus of openness and honesty—in the Buddhist perspective, lifting the deeper-than-conscious mechanisms out of the under-ground, out of the "tacit dimension" Michael Polanyi describes, freeing the stream of awareness that is always ebbing and flowing in everyone's experience. Meditation, pursued with rigor over the years, liberates individuals from unconscious and conscious compulsions, correcting nursery and glands and rearing. Insights, perceptions, memories of past and present are creatively synthesized in ways an adopted linguistic system, as in professionally specialized knowledge, prevent one from experiencing.

This is why Charles Hartshorne can characterize Buddhism as one of the two self-corrective communities of the modern world, the other being the community of modern science. Lacking this kind of self-corrective capability, it has always been difficult for men and women to trust their own power to act, to utter their own intuited lines. One of the major historians of Buddhism, A. Berriedale Keith, describes this "way of intuition" by saying that "it is essential and proper to develop the capacity for winning such visions, and this is and must be a matter for individual experience, and in it the autonomy of the individual successfully emerges from the constraint of authority in an experience which is essentially ineffable, however real it may be to him who experiences it."[6]

The horizons of every culture-world—held in place by pressures of social conformity, by the sharing of a single linguistic system, and by the presumptions of authority which in one way or another men and women have exercised over their fellow-creatures—are limits that Buddhism has called in question for twenty-five centuries in dozens of radically different cultures and civilizations. At the very center of Buddhism is the discovery that each individual has an enormous and almost wholly unexplored capability for enlarging and deepening awareness, vivifying and enriching the quality of

6. A. Berriedale Keith, *Buddhist Philosophy in India and Ceylon*, p. 39.

the passing moment, thus becoming more profoundly and memorably alive.

Buddhism is likewise the major adversary of the affluent society, unmistakably arguing that time and energy released through an automated technology can continue to be devoted to luxurious comfort and pleasure only at the cost of reversing the long evolutionary expansion in the valuing consciousness of humankind. The hard task of the immediate future, as Buddhists would say, is to extend this probing relationship still further, increasing and intensifying in people of all nations, races, social classes, and ethnic traditions the realization that this enrichment of the qualities they experience in their lives is both possible and necessary. Max Scheler has this in mind in the following words:

We have never before seriously faced the question whether the entire development of Western civilization, that one-sided and over-active process of expansion outward, might not ultimately be an attempt using unsuitable means—if we lose sight of the complementary art of inner self-control over our entire underdeveloped and otherwise involuntary psychological life, an art of meditation, search of soul, and forbearance. We must learn anew to envisage the great, invisible solidarity of all living beings in universal life, of all minds in the eternal spirit—and at the same time the mutual solidarity of the world process and the destiny of its supreme principle. And we must not just accept this world unity as a mere doctrine, but practice and promote it in our inner and outer lives.[7]

The chief aim of the Buddha's thought is to distinguish sharply a way in which individuals can extricate themselves from the suffering that results when the natural expansiveness and creativity of life are constrained and confined by artificial culture-worlds whose limits in the last resort are embedded in the self. In focusing attention upon the passing moment in its fullness, and upon the transitoriness of life, the

7. Quoted in *Buddhism in the Modern World*, ed. Heinrich Dumoulin, p. 321. It should be unnecessary to add that no Buddhist would speak, as Scheler does, of "envisaging the invisible solidarity of all minds in the eternal spirit."

Buddha struck at the tap root of humankind's propensity to cling to the one-sidedness and fragmentariness of life, since what has no independent existence loses its grip over the individual who is oriented to the richness of the fulfilled "now." All tendency to cling to the relative and the fragmentary vanishes when the impermanence of life has been disclosed.[8]

It is the present instant that is really real. Reality, as William James writes, "comes in drops." These "drops," or "unities of existence," these "occasions of experience," according to Whitehead, "are the really real things which in their collective unity compose the evolving universe, ever plunging into the creative advance."[9] Existence is momentary; at no two instants is any experience identical. T. R. V. Murti understands that "the Buddhist view reduces change to a series of entities emerging and perishing; each entity however rises and perishes in entirety; it does not become another. Movement for the Buddhist is not the passage of an entity from one point to another; it is the emergence, at appropriate intervals, of a series of entities, like the individual pictures of a 'movie' show; it is a series of full-stops."[10] Hartshorne applauds Buddhism for returning us to an honest empiricism in which "the concrete subjects are the momentary actualities."[11]

In reversing the role traditionally ascribed to culture-worlds and their almost universal strategies of rational support, and in turning individuals toward a rigorous adventure with a whole universe of *khanavāda* ("point-instants" or "momentary experiences"), the Buddha freed humanity from reliance upon established belief systems and mythologies that are today becoming undone. "The whole history of Buddhist philosophy," the eminent Russian scholar T. I. Stcherbatsky writes, "can be described as a series of attempts to penetrate more deeply

8. Ramanan, *Nāgārjuna's Philosophy*, p. 48. Cf. Govinda, *Psychological Attitude*, pp. 56–59.

9. Alfred North Whitehead, *Modes of Thought*, p. 151.

10. T. R. V. Murti, *The Central Philosophy of Buddhism*, p. 75. See also pp. 121, 175–177.

11. Charles Hartshorne, "The Buddhist-Whiteheadian View of the Self and the Religious Traditions," p. 301, pp. 298–302.

into this original intuition of Buddha, what he himself believed to be his great discovery."[12] Buddhist schools of philosophy wrestled for centuries with the implications of this perspective upon the infinite perfectibility of life, once the artificial superstructures and limits have been abandoned through meditation.[13]

The natural consequence of this process of enlightenment, the optimum degree of which was attained under the famous pipal tree at Bodhagayā twenty-five hundred years ago, is the sense of being deeply rooted in the living world of which one's own life is an entirely natural part. One stops using such common figures of speech as *"facing* reality," and acquires an intuitive sense of *"coming out* of this world" in the way leaves come from a tree. One's whole relation to the universe may undergo this sort of fundamental change.[14] Shifts such as these in linguistic habits accompany collateral shifts in the undergirding of one's life. Instead of asking with Immanuel Kant, How are synthetic a priori judgments possible? Buddhism faces the essential questions: How is it possible for men and women to emancipate themselves from the way they were reared, from the enticements of a consumership career, from exclusive memberships in race, creed, social class and nation, which make everyone a piece of mankind whose mythologically expressed pretensions cripple men and women in their capacity for experiencing life in its organic flow? How is it possible for individuals to free themselves (*and by example one another*) from the subtle conditioning process of lusting after the idolatry of *enrichissez-vous*, celebrating millionaires who have used their unrepeatable opportunities for qualitative enrichment in ways that reduce life to a simple struggle after wealth? How is it possible to center our lives in the unstructured, undifferentiated qualitative flow in which individuals become vitally and memorably alive?

12. T. I. Stcherbatsky, "The Soul Theory of the Buddhists," pp. 824–825.
13. R. Puligandla, "Could There Be an Essential Unity of Religions?" p. 19.
14. See Alan Watts, *The Book.*

This is the cultural legacy of millions on the continent of Asia who may find in the living Buddhist tradition (especially since their enthrallment with the West has ended) the only unifying force for the immediate future. The political forms will come later on, long after their enactment of the deepening personal synthesis and their vision of life's oneness have been in place. Scholars working in the Buddhist legacy, such as Father Thomas Berry of Fordham University, are sufficiently encouraged to believe that, as Berry asserts, "Buddhism is adapting to the urgencies of the present and exerting an influence on the shaping of the future, changing and in turn being changed as the human community undergoes a transformation such as it has never undergone since the rise of the higher civilizations some five thousand years ago."[15] According to Berry, the present encounter of Buddhism with the modern world is one of the "most exciting moments that [Buddhism] has ever seen, for it has become one of the most significant forces in the intellectual, spiritual, and aesthetic life of the contemporary world. Far from being in a state of absolute decline, it is in a state of resurgence."[16]

One of the discoveries now being made by men and women exploring the Buddhist orientation is the feeling of release and liberation from experiencing themselves as an alienated scrap of humanity blown by volatile change. There is a victory over this pathology of powerlessness which is widespread in the contemporary world. There is a new sense of personal power, a feeling of vitality with which the present-centered life is strangely infused (strange because it is very rare). Exploring their experience of what Malalasekera called "the fulfilled *Now*," they feel themselves in control of the way they choose to respond and able to change their minds as events may suggest.

It is for reasons such as these that one is apt to understand Buddhism in the fullest degree only by meeting it embodied in a person. One deficiency, indeed, of nearly all Buddhist

15. Thomas Berry, Rev. of *The Religious Life of Man*, pp. 239–240. See also his *Buddhism*.
16. Berry, Rev. of *Religious Life*, p. 241.

scholarship in the West is a natural expression of what Robert N. Bellah terms "the Greek cognitive bias"[17] running like a major artery through the corpus of Western civilization—it is the persuasion that Buddhism can be communicated in a book. In its highest priorities and values, as well as in its Buddhist scholarship, Western civilization follows its tendency to be a people of the book. The organic wholeness of experience is split into a world of language on the one hand and the living existential response of life on the other. In societies like Sri Lanka, on the contrary, the complaint is heard that Buddhism has languished in their land, less because of the coercive policies followed by British imperialism than from the lack of living *arahants*, the ideal embodiments of the Buddhist way. "It is no good," one Singhalese said, "just to read a book. You have to be taught by one who has the experience of the truth." There must be a living example for people to follow, in addition to the self-examination and meditation.

Adequately prepared by reading the actual teachings of the Buddha, having entered into the experience of the artistic and especially the architectural forms in which the tradition is expressed, and having participated in the discipline of meditation, one is ready to be carried to the deepest level of communication between East and West—the encounter with Buddhism alive. Ideas that may have been too ambiguous to grasp, and architectural themes that may have distorted and falsified the tradition, face their simple and straightforward test when enacted in the person-to-person encounter. It is here that qualities moving too quickly to permit inference or implication—the qualities that are the most intimate fact of life— may validate what is fraudulent in book or building. This concern with the living personality has always been a part of the Buddhist orientation to life, even going back, as G. C. Pande suggests, to the time of the Buddha himself:

A few individual traits of Buddha's personality stand out unmistakably. He was of a meditative turn of mind. His love of silence was most noticeable. His assemblies were free from noise. He rec-

17. Robert N. Bellah, *Beyond Belief.*

ommended to his disciples the Noble Silence. The compassionate nature of the Buddha has been famed down the ages, and it seems inconceivable that it should have been without a very real foundation in history. The independence of Buddha's character is another noticeable feature. He was opposed to dogmatism which he sought to replace by a profoundly based critical attitude. He recognised certain problems to be logically indeterminate and on these preserved silence. He was very practical. He wanted action and not mere speculation which can in no way lead one to the goal. The greatness of Buddha's personality is manifest from the fact that no other individual has left as strong an impress on the history of Indian culture as he.[18]

Over the centuries, this impact upon Indian culture was extended to the people of East Asia—China, Japan, Korea and Tibet—and to Southeast Asia, particularly Burma, Cambodia, Laos, Sri Lanka and Thailand. Despite all the cultural differences in so vast a region and across so large a period of time, the Buddha's presence has been very much on the minds of people of many diverse ethnic, racial, cultural and national backgrounds. Nowhere in all these regions of Asia is one for long without evidence of the Buddha's impact upon the art and architecture of the region and in the legacy of Buddhist teachings translated into twenty different languages of the immense region. "Scholars in the centers of learning," Thomas Berry writes, "popular preachers in the smallest villages, have read the same scriptural traditions, have commented on the same basic doctrines, centered the mind on the same person of the Buddha, quoted the same phrases, and worked out the same basic pattern of release from the impermanent, sorrowful, insubstantial world." The volume of translations is itself unequalled, Berry states, "in the history of cultural diffusion until modern times."[19]

Following Daisetz Suzuki's death, Thomas Merton joined many men and women in a memorial volume of *Eastern Buddhist*, in which he stressed the need to discover Buddhism "in an existential manner, in a person in whom it is alive; then

18. G. C. Pande, *Studies in the Origins of Buddhism*, pp. 391–393.
19. Berry, *Buddhism*, pp. 177, 130.

there is no longer a problem of understanding doctrines."[20] The point has been made again and again in the field work of everyone who has endeavored to investigate the Buddhist Way.

My own field work certainly bore this out to me in my encounters with the living personalities of Soen Ozeki and, later, of Taisen Deshimaru. Soen Ozeki proved to be one of the most remarkable individuals I have met, whether in Buddhist or non-Buddhist lands, and his reactions to the modern world were relevant for the research in which I was engaged in the summer of 1972, and are relevant now. His appeal to students of the highest academic qualifications gave the lie to observers who had long claimed, especially about Zen, that it is successful as a foreign export but that no one is interested in Buddhism in Japan. Students came to run with him at four o'clock in the morning, and they sang and danced with him on impulse. They sought him out individually because, as I discovered for myself, he had an unmistakable grasp of the suffering they were undergoing in the face of a volatile, impersonal, pressurized world.

One thing was truly remarkable. They did not come to learn Zen meditation, although he was the chief priest at Daitokuji, a compound of twenty-three affiliated temples. Ozeki taught his young visitors nothing about the *koan* or *zazen*, respectively the enigmatic Zen question and the seated meditation which Daisetz Suzuki had made famous over the years. When I tried to discover the source of his attraction to students, I discovered that he had nothing to tell them. The way he understood it, they came to be with someone for a little while who felt their suffering, who had confidence in them, and who especially had nothing to teach and no advice to give. He had boundless confidence that they already possessed the capabilities for solving their own problems. He had a healthy respect for the tenderness of life in the face of the senseless brutalities of this world.

20. Thomas Merton, "D. T. Suzuki: The Man and His Work," p. 6. See also his *Zen and the Birds of Appetite*.

It was the personal existential encounter, rather than any-thing communicated with words, that encouraged these students of Japan's world-famous university in Kyoto. A remarkable young roshi with a firm handshake and burning, compassionate eyes encouraged in them something their up-bringing had left out of account. He was responding sponta-neously to the changing situations of life, and the confidence he exuded seemed to reassure his young friends that they could shape their own lives and choose in the face of a world of compulsive habit-ridden routine. A tabloid newspaper being circulated at the time on both Otani and Kyoto campuses quoted Ozeki as saying: "Unless we can be happy in the new Japan, we would not be happy in the old Japan either. Since we are here now, we should live and solve the problems of the new Japan; every moment we have to try to do our best; that is the treasure man has."[21]

Soen Ozeki was as radical in his attitude toward religion as anyone I had ever met, and this is one reason why it is a mistake to think of Buddhism as a religion in the Western mode. He obviously spoke, not as a priest, despite the saffron robes and clean-shaven head, but as a human being. With no knowledge of Charles Kingsley's remark (made famous by Marx) about "the opiate of the people," or of Marx's charac-terization of religion as a pattern of avoidance, a pseudo-sun around which men and women revolve who are unable to re-volve around themselves, Ozeki agreed with all of these re-marks. Most of the temples of Japan, he said, were museum pieces, with priests spending their lives accepting fees for fu-nerals and the memorial services in the years that follow death. When I asked how he had come into this "business" (and I used the term deliberately), he explained that he had been born into a family of fifteen children where money was scarce, that he had not been intelligent enough to become a professor, and that money had attracted him to the priesthood. "Money was something I understood," he said, "and we needed it in so large a family."

21. *Kansai-Action*, June 10, 1972.

When I asked if he told his young friends these things, he very simply answered, without offense, "Of course." He also told them that "young people should be leading the culture and changing it, instead of thinking that they are here to serve it." The more I saw of the young roshi, the less I wondered at the tabloid news story with pictures that had attracted my attention on a campus noisy with loudspeakers calling for an end to the war in Vietnam. Buildings were disfigured with large calligraphy expressing the world's indignation at this new American war. Indeed, it became a bit more difficult to conduct my interviews with professors to whom I had written for an appointment several weeks before. In the context, Soen Ozeki stood out in a way one could never explain, because he was Buddhism alive, addressing himself to events no one could ever anticipate in advance. He *was* the Buddhist orientation to the momentary occasion. There is *never* anything more real. Small wonder that during the eleven years he had been chief priest at Daitokuji the young roshi, then perhaps thirty-eight, had acquired a reputation as a man of broad interests and vitality, conducting a radio program at five o'clock in the morning four days each week, where he devoted himself as always to practical problems people were facing, whether sex, pollution, or loneliness from moving to metropolitan Japan.

Visiting with the young roshi, it became obvious why so many have said of Zen Buddhism that it has always been transmitted from person to person, rather than from a book. As I came away from the first interview, in which not a word had been spoken about anything specifically Buddhist or Japanese, a young couple from India were waiting to see him for the second time. It was easy to imagine that in some remarkable way his young friends saw in him a new human type, a denationalized, noninstitutionalized, unclassifiable, recivilized individual who had managed to eradicate pseudoidentities and could therefore identify spontaneously with individuals across a broad spectrum of concerns. He embodied in every gesture an unlearned awareness that identities fabricated in accordance with age, sex, social class, race, vocation, and ethnic and national background belong to the childhood of the race and have become maladaptive in the contemporary world. The most important thing he said, which may not have been a very essential thing to say in the context, is that sensitive people, awakening to their suffering, freely admitting it into conscious awareness without distortion or suppression, can discover in themselves, without assistance from anyone, the barriers to the creativity deeply running in their experience—and that "Every moment we must try." It was a forceful authentication of the Buddhist encounter with the contemporary world. Students looking absentmindedly for some way to withdraw from the frustrations of contemporary life were being told, chiefly with his nonverbal enactment, that the culture of the superindustrial age was made by human beings and that, as he was quoted in the tabloid, "no one should permit it to rule over him."

A diversion from a tight schedule of interviews in Tokyo, similar to the one that had brought me to Soen Ozeki, led me into the company of another Zen roshi—which is very strange indeed since my research has always been in the mainstream philosophy of the Buddhist tradition and only incidentally in Zen.[22] Professor Hajime Nakamura arranged for me to see the roshi, who was scheduled to return in a day or two to France, where he had formed the Association Zen d'Europe. When I arrived for the interview, I was ushered into an impressive four-storied white brick building, bearing the name Shinri-kenkyūjo—"Institute for Research Into Truth"—which had been donated by admirers for the probing and planning of Taisen Deshimaru. Now in his fifties, Deshimaru had overcome resistance from every quarter, the first from his Zen Master, Roshi Sawaki, who had counseled him not to become a priest at all but had finally ordained him. Everyone in authority at Sojiji, the "Vatican" of eighteen thousand Soto Zen temples in Japan, had opposed Deshimaru's mission to France from the beginning. He overcame all opposition. It had never been enough for him to take up life as a priest in some local

22. See comments comparing Theravāda with Zen in Nolan Pliny Jacobson, *Buddhism*, pp. 105–108.

temple, after the rigorous training at Sojiji, in the face of a world moving from one crisis to the next, possessed of thermonuclear warheads thousands of times more destructive than the bombs dropped on Hiroshima and Nagasaki. He had begun his European work in 1968, and in four years every major city of Western Europe had its first authentic center for Zen meditation and instruction.

Hoping that people of the West would grasp what he came to say in the forms of articulate speech, Deshimaru had first hired a lecture hall and planned a program of talk. But too few came to justify using an auditorium for his communication. He rented a vacant store window, and proceeded, in the Zen vernacular, "to sit."

Those who stopped to see what was going on in the window stood unbelieving at the sight of a man with a bull neck suitable for the wrestling ring sitting clean-shaven and bald, back straight as a poker, looking directly with half-closed eyes upon a bare wall. His face had the look of one who was thinking of nothing, which in Paris meant nothing at all. Looking at nothing, thinking of nothing—what in the world was happening in this store window? No one had ever seen anything like it in Paris. Day after day the big man sat in his saffron robe facing the blank wall in the window of an empty shop. The curious brought their friends to see the strange man who was doing nothing at all, for reasons no one could imagine.

That is the way Taisen Deshimaru brought Zen to Western Europe. Meditating before passing pedestrians confronted Parisians with a puzzle. To satisfy their curiosity they came face to face with a large man and a raspy voice, and eventually everyone found himself "sitting." Newcomers were asked, "Will you sit?" and they were on their way.

After my own initial interview with Deshimaru, I was invited to his farewell party the following day, where more than a hundred of all ages crowded into an upper room to show their support for his continuing mission to Paris, eating together a catered meal, then rising one by one to speak words of praise for the man who was helping the modern world discover the deep, unspeakable richness hidden customarily by the undigestible word. It was an unforgettable event lasting many hours, and it prepared me for the remarks of Paul Chauchard, opening the Fourth Congress of the International College of Psychosomatic Medicine in Kyoto in September 1977, to the effect that he had been working with Taisen Deshimaru for several years seeking a new understanding of health. Here, again, East was meeting West at the deepest level of mutual understanding, for the discovery of one's organic unity with the totality of life has been the central concern of Zen for centuries. As Dr. Yujiro Ikemi, Chairman of the Fourth Congress, observed in his paper at the meeting: "Zen Buddhism aims primarily at the full awakening of the total being to human existence. The process requires great humility and courage and cannot be approached only through ego-related conceptual thinking, but through a holistic way of thinking based on body feeling of 'Taitoku' which means understanding through the body, which frees us to live in the present moment, the 'Here and Now', to be creative, and to love unconditionally."[23]

Cross-cultural interchange, such as that of Chauchard, the French neurophysiologist, with Deshimaru, finds in the Buddhist tradition encouraging insights and perspectives. Robert E. Ornstein believes that in terms of this interchange "we are now on the threshold of a new understanding of man and his consciousness, one which might unite the scientific, objective, external approach of Western civilization and the personal, inward disciplines of the East. In many areas people are beginning to feel that we have left something (without knowing what) out of our cultural upbringing, out of our science, medicine, education, and personal development."[24] This probe toward a more adequate, complete, holistic appreciation of the experienced moment in its living matrix carries the highest priority in the work of R. D. Laing as well.

The most serious objection to the technical vocabulary currently used to describe psychiatric patients [Laing writes] is that it consists of words which split man up verbally in a way which is analo-

23. Dr. Ikemi's opening lecture, unpublished, Sept. 5, 1977.
24. Robert E. Ornstein, *The Mind Field*, pp. ix, 5.

gous to the existential splits we are seeking to understand. *But we cannot give an adequate account of the existential splits unless we can begin from the concept of a unitary whole, and no such concept exists,* nor can any such concept be expressed within the current language system of psychiatry or psycho-analysis. The words of the current technical vocabulary either refer to man in isolation from the other and the world, or they refer to falsely substantialized aspects of this isolated entity.[25]

As may be discerned from the phrase "falsely substantialized aspects," Laing has been searching for new perspectives in Buddhist traditions for many years, meeting with Nyānaponika Mahāthera in Sri Lanka and with Buddhist leaders in Thailand and Japan, looking for ways to combat the tensions that threaten daily to break out into open savagery in recurring monetary, military, moral and manic problems of the superindustrial age.

Hundreds and perhaps thousands of people—such as Thomas Merton, Robert Ornstein, Yujiro Ikemi, Paul Chauchard, Erich Fromm, and R. D. Laing—represent the most powerful effort of the contemporary world to assist the individual in our time to acquire "a sense of his presence in the world as a real, alive, whole, continuous person; as such, he can live out into the world and meet others: a world and others experienced as equally real, alive, whole, and continuous."[26] Laing's probing of the Buddhist legacy is illustrated in one of his poems:

> *Although innumerable beings have been led to Nirvana*
> *no being has been led to Nirvana*
> Before one goes through the gate
> one may not be aware there is a gate
> One may think there is a gate to go through
> and look for a long time for it without finding it
> One may find it and it may not open
> If it opens one may be through it
> As one goes through it
> one sees that the gate one went through
> was the self that went through it

25. R. D. Laing, *The Divided Self*, p. 17.
26. Ibid., p. 40.

> no one went through a gate
> there was no gate to go through
> no one ever found a gate
> no one ever realized there was never a gate.[27]

One day humankind may become whole, and wholly one. This is the ancient dream. They will meet in the crossroads and they will say to one another, "Come on in." This strangely ancient dream has become a necessity in the contemporary world, for reasons to which we must now turn.

27. R. D. Laing, *Knots*, p. 85.

3

⌇⌇⌇⌇⌇⌇⌇⌇⌇⌇⌇⌇⌇⌇⌇⌇⌇⌇⌇⌇⌇⌇⌇⌇⌇⌇⌇⌇⌇⌇⌇

The Central Conception
of Buddhism

It was reserved for the present century to give birth to the out-and-out assertion in systematic form that reality *is* process, and that laws as well as all things develop in the process of unceasing change. The modern Heraclitean is Alfred North Whitehead, but he is Heraclitus with a change. The doctrine of the latter, while it held that all things flow like a river and that change is so continuous that a man cannot step into the same river even once (since it changes as he steps), nevertheless also held that there is a fixed order which controls the ebb and flow of the universal tide.

> *John Dewey*
> *Time and Individuality*

The Buddhist said that even the unity through time of a physical thing, animal, or person covered an ultimate multiplicity of momentary states or "flashes" of reality. Here, and not in Heraclitus, was the emergence of a radical philosophy of process. For one thing, from the Greek we have some epigrams, from Buddha and his followers, a library.

> *Charles Hartshorne*
> *Creative Synthesis and*
> *Philosophic Method*

THE ENTIRE HISTORY of Buddhist theory and practice is in large part a series of efforts to penetrate more deeply into the central intuition of the Buddha, an intuition he experienced on the occasion of his world-famous Enlightenment. It was this Awakening that the Buddha, Stcherbatsky writes, "believed to be his great discovery."[1] This discovery made it possible for him to live in full view of the suffering of the whole world, with compassion for everything and everyone, without being thrown off balance by anything he saw.

The early teachings tell how his father sought to dissuade him from leaving on what appeared to be the quest of an irresponsible dreamer. According to early accounts, the Buddha tells his father that he will gladly renounce his "noble quest" if only the father can assure the son that the misfortunes he sees happening to others will not befall him and his father as well. He asks if his father can promise that his son will be free from suffering and death, from the anguish of a creature whose identity is forever in doubt, from the compulsive striving and general drivenness of life that strips the mind of its potential power "to work out its own salvation with diligence." From everything the Buddha sees, humanity appears to be the victim of insatiable needs. "Tell me, Father, that I shall be free of all this, and I will remain."

It was obvious to the Buddha that even the most clever and adaptable people spend their lives forever taking leave and that they sooner or later face changes to which they appear unable to adjust. To be independent in the vicissitudes of life, with confidence and personal identity despite old age and death, new penetrations must be achieved which had hitherto eluded the human creature. Pathological degrees of rigidity and inflexibility before unwanted change rise to dominance as life is normally lived; countless defensive strategies carry the self toward an eventual encounter with despair. In the effort to be master of its own house, human personality has a natural bent for allowing some specific goal or demand to rise to dominance over the total organism with all its native endowments. Within the psychosomatic system some poorly understood passion or drive is always taking the whole system under control, narrowing the range of attention.

1. T. I. Stcherbatsky, "The Soul Theory of the Buddhists," pp. 824–825. See also his small book, *The Central Conception of Buddhism and the Meaning of the Word 'Dharma'*, pp. 22–25, 40–41, 62–63.

The central conception stemming from the Buddha's personal struggle has been clarified by controversy between rival philosophical schools during the centuries following his Indian ministry of forty-five years. This conception is a unifying awareness of what is really real in the fleeting momentary now. It is not a form of intellectual understanding elaborated over the centuries into a systematic theory of humanity and the rest of nature. It is, rather, a penetrating intuition into the nature of the life process itself. As such, it is not something that the culture-world or symbolic system can confer upon anyone, or that one person can acquire from another. Whatever understanding may be won is itself a part of humankind's potential capacity, as a part of the life process, to become self-illuminating and free from their compulsions. To pursue intellectual understanding, for whatever light it can throw, is to disregard the organic unity of a person's interpenetrating powers. One looks in vain for a Buddhist *sutra* from which the meaning of life can simply be acquired by frequent and careful reading.

In relation to the manyness of experience in its deeper-than-linguistic concreteness, the insight and intuitive penetration are *one*. Murti calls this *Prajñā* ("nonconceptual intellectual intuition"), "the fruition of the practical and religious consciousness," and even "the *summum bonum* of all endeavor."[2]

There is never any expectation in Buddhism of acquiring a conceptual system in which the deepest secrets of life are explained. No Buddhist has ever provided a manual for living which describes and explains the entirety of nature as though from a lofty transcendental position. "If it were otherwise," Kenneth K. Inada writes, "Buddhism would easily fall into a system of absolute First Principles and there would be no challenge to understanding the empirically grounded existential strains in our everyday lives; there would be no meaning to the enthusiasm for the search for the basis of life itself."[3] Guenther emphasizes the point more strongly still: "Life be-

2. T. R. V. Murti, *The Central Philosophy of Buddhism*, p. 142.
3. Kenneth K. Inada, *Nāgārjuna*, p. 10.

comes meaningless only when this pursuit of meaning comes to an end; final meanings about which the authorities on eternal verities are so cocksure have mostly no meaning at all."[4] It goes without saying that the perspective cannot be won apart from a personal struggle in and with the web of conventional wisdom, penetrating from time to time into the nurturing matrix, as E. R. Sarathchandra phrases it, "individually known in the depths of one's being,"[5] free at last from compulsive clinging to specific entities in life's flow.

The central conception of Buddhism is thus a unifying awareness affecting the total organism with all its possibilities and endowments, an awareness of what is really real in each fleeting, momentary now. Buddhist philosophy has been preoccupied with causality throughout its history in the different cultures of Asia, but the uniqueness of the Buddhist stance resides in the fact that causality has never been an inducement to look briefly at a present fact or experience and then "quickly turn to its antecedents," as Allen Wheelis complains, "as to the conditions and influences from which it may have been derived." Continuing his criticism of "Western" science, Wheelis argues that "the hypnotic fascination with causality turns our heads, we look backwards. So the past is augmented at the expense of the present. We explain things by their origins."[6] People reared in Buddhist orientations never look backward for their roots, thinking to find their identities in their beginnings, nor, for that matter, do they look forward to some final consummatory end. The present alone manifests the full nature of existence. An important argument in Wheelis' recent book, *The End of the Modern Age*, could have been written by any Buddhist philosopher over the past two thousand years:

We have attention, curiosity, creativity, in but limited amount; in the Modern Age a large part of this vital force is withdrawn from

4. Herbert V. Guenther, *Philosophy and Psychology in the Abhidharma*, p. 134.
5. E. R. Sarathchandra, *Buddhist Psychology of Perception*, p. 102.
6. Allen Wheelis, *The End of the Modern Age*, pp. 70–71.

the trembling leaf, from the smell of a rose, from the mouth of a girl, from the dancing feet. In the interest of power we are forever looking back, picking among the ruins for causes. We would rather control the world than experience it, and to this end will sacrifice anything, everything, life itself.[7]

From the tradition's emergence in India twenty-five centuries ago, Buddhist philosophers have recognized that our lives must be forever threatened with meaninglessness unless a more correct view of causality can be won. "In the Nikāyas," K. N. Jayatilleke writes, "causality plays a central role. 'He who sees the nature of causation sees the dhamma (i.e. the teaching) and he who sees the dhamma sees the nature of causation.' It is claimed to be the truth about the universe discovered by the Buddha in the final stage of his enlightenment."[8]

In its central conception, to which we must now turn our attention, Buddhism has sought to lead men and women to the nexus of concrete existence, the deeper-than-linguistic vitality and power in which human life acquires its identity, its unlimited adaptability to change, and its ability to live in the vivid qualitative flow where life is responding to life. It is to this deeper-than-cultural foundation, beyond the frontiers of social and conscious existence, that the Buddha "awakened" beneath the pipal tree at Bodhagayā six years after leaving his father's home. Buddhism, indeed, *is* a process of recovering this central intuition from beneath the almost impenetrable layers of personal defilement and the tenacious superstructures of conventional belief with which human communities are always seeking to control behavior. The name, *Buddhism*, comes from the Sanskrit root *budh*, meaning to become aware, and to know. As layer upon layer of misdirection are exposed, one becomes confirmed in the affirmation with which the *Dhammapada* opens: "All that we are is the result of what we have thought."

Such is the basic perspective in all Buddhist traditions whether Theravāda, Mahāyāna, or even Vajrayana (Tibetan)

7. Ibid., pp. 71–72.
8. K. N. Jayatilleke, *Early Buddhist Theory of Knowledge*, p. 454.

Buddhism, revealing what Inada calls "the psycho-physical continuum throughout the whole of being,"[9]—the ground or matrix of our thinking process, only rarely if ever taken into account in the common life.

THE ULTIMATE UNDERSTANDING

Buddhist philosophy has sought with astonishing perseverance to appreciate and in some small measuure to understand the all-encompassing aesthetic fullness that gives unity to life. Fleeting glimpses of the fundamental nature of reality are won. It is a process of *paṭicca-samuppāda* ("creative coorigination"). It heals men and women of their self-encapsulation in *tanhā* ("craving"), *māna* ("conceit"), and *diṭṭhi* ("false views"), three features of what in Pali is called *papañca*, sometimes interpreted as "conceptual proliferation." The root causes of the self-encapsulation can also be formulated by another "evil trinity"—*lobha*, *doṣa*, and *moha* ("greed," "hatred," "delusion").

The central intuition is this: the world that exists is the result of the *nonexistence* of any independent substance. Creative experience is *all there is*. What is completely real is *process*, whether our field of investigation be the interactions of elementary particles of high energy physics, the cells in which the DNA molecule is found, or the singular events of the fleeting moments of each day where we experience the varied wonder of this world. There is always the *becoming* of ever-new events, in the doctrine called *anicca*, the transitoriness of life. The *Abhidhamma* concentrates on the notion of a "stream

9. Inada, *Nāgārjuna*, p. 18. See also U Thittila, "The Fundamental Principles of Theravāda Buddhism." Thittila, the leading monk in Rangoon, writes: "The understanding of dependent origination is basic to an understanding of Buddhism" (p. 81). See also Hajime Nakamura, "Interrelational Existence": "According to the thought of early Buddhism, the way to deliverance from suffering taught by the Buddha is nothing other than the right knowledge of the truth of dependent origination" (p. 110). Nakamura refers especially to *The Book of the Kindred Sayings* (*Saṃyutta-Nikāya*), vol. 2, pp. 78–79, and *The Middle Length Sayings* (*Majjhima-Nikāya*), vol. 1, pp. 262–263; vol. 3, pp. 3–13.

of existence," the central feature being its theory of *khaṇika-vāda* ("momentariness"), the analysis here resembling White-head's "throbbing actualities," "puffs of existence," or "pulsa-tions of experience."[10]

One of the most productive Buddhist scholars says that it is precisely because of this living juxtaposition and succession of events in their momentariness that the possibility exists of becoming free from our compulsions and distortions. The con-cept of relational origination, Govinda writes, "shows itself as the necessary counterpart of the anattā-idea, the doctrine of no soul or substantial self which emphasizes the character of life and growth, in contrast to the fossilized concept of an ab-solute entity which would logically call for similarly absolute (lifeless) laws."[11]

Hartshorne, the contemporary American philosopher who inherits most fully the Buddhist perspective, writes that "en-during substances in a living world constitute an elemental confusion contrary to both logic and life, a fact taken into ac-count by countless Buddhists for two thousand years, some of whom at least were constructive metaphysicians."[12] And fur-ther, "Perhaps at long last we should join the Buddhists in recognizing that an enduring individual is a society or se-quence of occasions" rather than a soul-substance to which the qualities of a life-time adhere. Hartshorne, further, makes an essential distinction when he concludes that "personal identity through experiences is a property of the experiences, they are not properties of the identity, or of the ego. Egocen-tric motivations essentially consist in metaphysical confu-sion."[13]

This is precisely what the Buddha taught. "Which now," he asked one day, "is thy true self, that of yesterday, that of

10. Bhikkhu J. Kashyap, *The Abhidhamma Philosophy*, pp. 165–166.
11. Lama Anagarika Govinda, *The Psychological Attitude of Early Buddhist Philosophy*, pp. 56–57.
12. Charles Hartshorne, *Creative Synthesis and Philosophic Method*, pp. 87–88.
13. Charles Hartshorne, "Personal Identity from A to Z," p. 214; idem, Introduction to *Philosophers of Process*, pp. xii, xix.

today, or that of tomorrow, for the preservation of which thou dost clamor?" Anyone clinging to the structured self as substance was said by the Buddha to be "writhing in delusion."[14] Hartshorne continues in the Buddhist vein:

The basic motivation is neither the appeal of a self for that same self; nor even the appeal of other selves for the own self. Rather, it is something more general and yet, in its instances, more specific or concrete: *the appeal of life for life*—thus my past or future life (or self) for my present life or self and also the appeal of your past or future life (or the lives of birds, or the cosmic life) for your or my present life, reality, or self. Apparently it was Buddha who discovered this, centuries before . . . Christ rediscovered it.[15]

The deepest penetrations of reason inform us, according to the Buddha, that we are not merely human, not merely man and woman, but also sunlight, river, sky and sea, and all that lives in the depths of the oceans and in the farthest reaches of the ecosphere. To be reasonable means to embrace, to nurture and be nurtured by, this larger web of life. The power of encompassing a widening range of creation is a power we share as human creatures with everyone and everything that lives. The voice of reason in us is the voice of a world alive.

Society is more fundamental in the Buddhist orientation than substance. Nothing can have an independent existence; nothing has a self-established nature. No unconditioned substance, no soul or self or Being, or Nature, or Universe-at-large, or Truth has any place in the Buddhist view. The most famous illustration of this in Buddhist literature occurs in the dialogues between a Buddhist sage, Nāgasena, and King Menander, one of Alexander's successors who held sway over Northwest India following Alexander's death. In the document *Questions of King Milinda*, Nāgasena tells the monarch that the chariot is made up of wheels and axle and other parts, a society of interrelated features, just as a house or army or city is likewise a society of elements disposed toward one another in the unity of function. If you infer a chariot

14. See Paul Carus, *The Gospel of Buddha*, pp. 138–139.
15. Hartshorne, *Creative Synthesis*, pp. xx–xxi.

behind the parts, as causally operative upon the parts, and a similar entity behind a man or kingdom or house, you must infer such an entity behind every event or thing.[16] The issue haunts the history of Western philosophy. In the *Parmenides* we see Plato struggling to resolve the issue in a way that calls his entire metaphysical system into question. Whitehead's position supports the Buddhist point of view: "There is no going behind actual entities to find anything more real."[17]

Denial of substance is a central Buddhist position through the ages. The life process becomes more intelligible in the concept of conditioned genesis, or relational origination, or what Nakamura and Suzuki prefer to call "the interrelatedness of all things." The familiar formula is *pratītya-samutpāda*, or, in Pali, *paṭicca-samuppāda*. Every moment in the process depends upon every preceding moment for its emergence, and the passing moment with its new choices and possibilities "originates" the next. As Whitehead again and again has it: "The way the past perishes is the way the future becomes."

Each *dhamma* ("moment") inherits along innumerable lines, synthesizing the relevant qualities into a world that is creative in every cell. Each such organic unity is like a work of art in the wholeness it confers on every part, and the serenity the confirmed Buddhist finds in such "pulsations of experience" is the same serenity the art lover finds in great art. The movement in this process of the "many" into the eminent "one" of the fulfilled now is the rhythm of the universe as an organic whole.

Nāgārjuna opens his *Mūlamadhyamakakārikā* with the verse:

At nowhere and at no time can entities ever exist by originating out of themselves, from others, from both (self-other), or from the lack of causes.[18]

The same verse is translated by another scholar as follows:

16. Quoted in various sources, e.g. Louis de la Vallee Poussin, *The Way to Nirvana*, pp. 42–43.
17. Alfred North Whitehead, *Process and Reality*, pp. 27–28.
18. Quoted in Inada, *Nāgārjuna*, p. 39.

There is no entity anywhere that arises from itself, from another, from both (itself and another), or by chance.[19]

To guarantee the absence of either material or spiritual substratum, Nāgārjuna closes his opening chapter with the verses:

The effect (i.e., arisen entity) has the relational condition but the relational conditions have no self-possessing (natures). How can an effect, arising from no self-possessing (natures), have the relational condition?
Consequently, the effect (i.e. arisen entity) is neither with relational nor without non-relational condition. Since the effect has no existing status, wherein are the relational and non-relational conditions?[20]

The basic aim of Nāgārjuna is to clarify the formula of *pratītya-samutpāda* (in Pali, *paṭicca-samuppāda*), the Buddha's distinctive perspective in which the full creativity of the present moment is meticulously preserved.[21]
Many centuries ago the Buddhists had concluded that humanity has no realistic option except to participate as fully as possible in the creativity always incarnate in what Malalasekera prefers to call "the fulfilled *Now*." A universal concept, Malalasekera contends, refers to "an infinite number of discrete, evanescent elements in a state of ceaseless activity or commotion, in a state of perpetual becoming." Put another way, "creative forces," Herbert Guenther writes, are all that exist.[22] Everyone not completely imprisoned in what is pathological—from a Buddhist perspective—has the possibility of feeling the extensive continuum of the world at large. Everyone maintaining an awareness of each moment's novel forms

19. Alex Wayman, "Who Understands the Four Alternatives of the Buddhist Texts?" p. 10. See also Ives Waldo, "Nāgārjuna and Analytic Philosophy."
20. Quoted in Inada, *Nāgārjuna*, p. 42.
21. Ibid., p. 38. It is the "most essential and central concept," Inada writes, commanding with the concept of the Middle Path of the historical Buddha "the greatest philosophical and religious attention from all Buddhists" ("The Ultimate Ground of Buddhist Purification," pp. 43, 45, 53).
22. Gunapala Piyasena Malalasekera, "Aspects of Reality Taught by Theravāda Buddhism," p. 78; Guenther, *Philosophy and Psychology*, p. 241.

of togetherness has the choice of participating in events in-completely determined in advance. The world is alive to its microscopic depths; creativity is the pattern of its life. The only terminus is everywhere, in the fulfilled momentary now, and in each now a previous many are being creatively altered to become One, a new form of togetherness in the extensive continuum of the world at large.

The Oneness forever transforms the past, which is always a constituent in whatever is happening now. The synthesis of old and new is always new. Each novel one, having "become," takes its place in the new many to serve as constituents in a fresh form of novel togetherness. What is in the world at any moment, therefore, was not in its previous states.

The Buddhist process of relational origination, it should be emphasized, never culminates in the sort of consummation symbolized by a Supreme Being in which everything—and everyone—is finally fulfilled in a terminal manner. In the Buddhist view creativity never ceases. The opposite of crea-tivity is not the *absence* of it, for this is impossible: the oppo-site is *suffering*, which is where we are when we begin to re-flect upon our life in the world.

The Buddhist struggle has been to remain positively open and openly committed to the only reality there ever is, what alone is really real—the moment in which the flower is at an unprecedented stage of blooming, where the preceding stages of experienced togetherness (or relational origination) are surpassed forevermore.

The aim of life at the human level, consequently, is to free oneself from being possessed by any technique, any habitual perspective or deed, any social class orientation or resent-ment, any greed or lust or delusion, any specialized knowl-edge however valid, any image of self or others, in order that the fullness of quality rising and ebbing in the natural rhythm of the world's life may be free to infuse the human system with the novel qualities of the now. To the extent that individ-uals and social groups live without this awareness—this in-sight into the way freedom and order mutually sustain a cre-ative world—they become captives of their own self-serving and self-isolating strategies, adopt the mentality of the predator whose survival is always endangered in a creative world, and nudge the human adventure toward some fraudulent principle of authority with which we can never wholeheartedly identify our lives.

The whole of Buddhist thought is permeated with this perspective on the creativity incarnate in the fleeting now. The Buddhist term for these truly singular events is *khaṇa-vāda* or, in Pali, *kṣaṇa-vāda*, moments in what might be called a microprocess of millions of daily experiences beyond the grasp of memory and the relatively gross scale and measure of perception. In his widely read inquiry into Western interpretations of Nirvana, Guy Welbon confirms what we have been saying, that "creativity pervades both the way and the goal of Buddhism," and that "ignoring its presence would be to imperil any attempt to understand the Buddhist Nirvāna." We would also be neglecting the one unambiguous distinction, Welbon further writes, "between Buddhism and Hinduism in most of its forms."[23]

All of these writers on Buddhism perceive and emphasize precisely what the only major American philosopher with extensive knowledge of Buddhism, Charles Hartshorne, has written: "For a philosophy of becoming, basic terms like 'reality', 'truth', 'what there is', the 'universe', 'what is going on', really mean reality as of now, the truth now, what there is now, the universe now, what is going on now (as conditioned by whatever has already gone on)—or else they have no unambiguous meaning."[24] Creative synthesis is "what is going on" in these momentary nows. And Guenther confirms that this "is the Buddhist conception of the unconditional realness of what there is."[25] This is what the Buddhists have been saying for centuries, as Hartshorne well knows:

> Experience of emergent synthesis feeds on its own previous products, and on nothing else whatever! This is the 'ultimacy' of

23. Guy Richard Welbon, *The Buddhist Nirvana and Its Western Interpreters*, p. 304.
24. Hartshorne, *Creative Synthesis*, p. 17.
25. Herbert V. Guenther, *Buddhist Philosophy in Theory and Practice*, p. 19.

creativity. Sharing of creativity is the social character of experience, its aspect of sympathy, participation, identification with others. Moreover, even one's own past self is strictly speaking, 'another'—as hundreds of thousands of Buddhists have, for over a score of centuries, been trying to tell the world. I hold that in this they have simply been accurate. One can regard one's past self with love, but also with antipathy, much as one can the selves of other persons. Sheer identity or sheer non-identity [as Govinda has been quoted previously as saying] cannot be the correct account of this matter.[26]

For Buddhism, all entities including humans are social in nature, each the emergent synthesis of another now, each inheriting the "ripening fruit" of the past, and all constituting a special society whose members may never be physiologically present to one another but are nevertheless internally related in ways mere contiguity could hardly provide.[27] The Buddha's most widely known definition of a human being follows from this: "Each is the heir of his own actions" (*Dhammapada*). *Karma* and creativity are but different terms for the same emergent synthesis in the now. We become participants in the unpredictable legacy of tomorrow when we break the grip of the habit-ridden encapsulated self.

The responsibility Buddha here imposes upon us is to perceive that the world is not mastered by self-mortification, nor by ritual or ceremony, nor by avoidance and withdrawal, nor by serving the wants of the encapsulated self, regardless of how "enlightened" this self may be. Our responsibility is to perceive that freedom and existence are but two aspects of the same relational origination. The free act of experiencing is the universal principle of what is really real.

The Buddha discovered the feature that has given man not only his central responsibility but his distinctive niche in the economy of nature: there is no apparent limit to the capacity of the human creature for acquiring new increments of quality and adding to the aesthetic richness and vitality of life—no limit except those he imposes, in his compulsive striving and

26. Hartshorne, *Creative Synthesis*, p. 8.
27. See Nolan Pliny Jacobson, *Buddhism*, pp. 126ff.

ignorance, upon himself. Nothing can take the place of the individual's own private war against what Buddhists call "the four overpowering forces" and "the three basic ills" which constitute the contagion afflicting the human order of life.

In the light of the long commitment of Western philosophy to a substratum or substance of one sort or another, such as Locke's unknown substratum to which all the qualities of sensory experience adhere, the heightened interest in Buddhism in our time represents a cultural breakthrough unexcelled in the entire history of philosophy. Creativity, or "creative synthesis," as he prefers to say, was first clearly formulated, Hartshorne believes, "by the Buddhists, with their 'no-soul, no-substance' doctrine, a doctrine to which modern thought has finally found its way with the growing prominence of Whiteheadian thought. . . . Actual entities are experiences functioning as objects for subsequent experiences, which may or may not belong to the same personal stream of consciousness." "This," he concludes, "is Whitehead's profoundly original discovery anticipated only in ancient Buddhism."[28]

Creativity is "that principle by which the many, which are the universe disjunctively, become the one actual occasion, which is the universe conjunctively. It lies in the nature of things that the many enter into the complex unity. The many become one, and are increased by one."[29] This formulation by Whitehead is precisely the relational origination Nāgārjuna discusses in the first verse of his *Mūlamadhyamakakārikā* in the passage that is so important it deserves to be quoted a second time:

There is no entity anywhere that arises from itself, from another, from both (itself and another), or by chance.

The first principle of Buddhism (and of Whitehead) is that of "creative process." Creativity is the unlimited, ultimate, inexplicable stuff of the universe; it is the cure for what Heidegger called "the homelessness of modern man." It is able alone to cope, therefore, with those compulsive pathologies

28. Charles Hartshorne, *Whitehead's Philosophy*, pp. 5, 130.
29. Alfred North Whitehead, *Process and Reality*, pp. 31–32.

that only the earth can cure. Buddhism is humankind's most persevering effort to participate in the creativity incarnate in the passing now.

Creativity, then, is the universal feature of a world that is alive in every pore. Everything that happens is limited in its freedom only by the freedom of everything else. The future continues to be our own happening, the outcome of deeds we enact along the way. As we come to understand this, we face the option of impoverishing life in submission to what we and others want or have concluded about the world, or of enacting the more generous future, improvising as we go. When we forget that reflection and analysis occur in the midst of creation, we become trapped in pathological states of trying to manipulate the ultimate momentum of life in the interest of some design determined in advance. It is significant that one of the ancient teachings, found in the *Saṃyutta-Nikāya*, speaks of being freed from just such "snares" by the dynamic vector character of events with their *anukampati* ("vibrating after or towards"); this is, indeed, the literal meaning of Buddhist compassion.[30] Far from being wholly or even chiefly a matter of conscious intent, compassion is an intrinsic feature of events themselves as they attain in their togetherness some un-precedented and unpredictable form.

This interrelatedness among individuals, each being the shepherd of many lives, constitutes the basis for "infinite compassion," the special legacy of Buddhism to the contemporary world. One is a participant in all that lives, or has lived, or will live, regardless of whatever our conscious minds may fail to acknowledge. There is no other way of perceiving oneself in the deepest reality-oriented sense. Once illusions are swept away, the immanence of the past is found energizing in the present. The illustration closest to us is probably our own bodies, whose functions are occasions for energy transference

30. *Book of the Kindred Sayings (Saṃyutta-Nikāya)*, vol. 1, pp. 131–132. The dynamic vector character of Whitehead's "actual entities" prehending other entities in the production of "novel forms of togetherness" is a technical modern formulation of the "creative forces" which are "vibrating after or toward" and hence translated as "compassion."

stretching into the environment far beyond the limits of imagination. Early Buddhism, in particular, placed this kind of emphasis upon the role of the human body. Life for the Buddhist becomes meaningless only when, beginning with his life in the body, his widening participation comes to a dead end. "To be and to remain alive," as Guenther interprets the early Buddhist texts, "we must not allow ourselves to be carried into some shallow back-water."[31] Unless we feel the creative matrix of energy *alive in us each moment*, we are out of touch with what is most real in our existence. All forms of Buddhist meditation, from *Satipaṭṭhāna* to *Mettā* to *Zazen*, have as their purpose to restore awareness of this creative matrix.

One consequence of this Buddhist perspective is that men and women reared under its influence rarely generate the feelings of rootlessness, estrangement, and pathological loss of identity so prominent in the experience of Western people during the past century or more. Buddhism has resources for preventing the cul-de-sac of ontological emptiness and nihilism. Each throb of existence has some value for itself, for others, and for the rest of nature. Creativity is never threatened with meaninglessness and despair. Successful penetration through meditation of Saṃuṛti-Satya ("the covered and clouded nature of things") gives people the sense of being unrepeatable actualities in a life that is forever new.

The prizing of the unity of the momentary experience, no element of which has *svabhāva* ("self-established nature"), tends also to produce the tolerant, compassionate, joyful, nonviolent, tranquil individuals often encountered in the different culture-worlds of Burma, Sri Lanka, and Japan, as all have observed who have lived there for extended periods of time. As but one example, I met during my stay in Rangoon an American professor who, after two years in a community-development project in Iran, could scarcely believe the gladness in the faces of people loitering along the avenues of the large metropolitan center. It is reasonable to suspect that it is the Buddhist influence within the diverse traditions of Ja-

31. Guenther, *Philosophy and Psychology*, pp. 134, 229.

pan that leads people there to reflect the attitude of one group of professors meeting in a seminar in the Tokyo area, one member of which made the comment: "We Japanese do not *believe* in religion, we *enjoy* it!" And the room was filled with laughter.

Interfused with local ways of thinking wherever it has spread since its origin in India twenty-five centuries ago, this Buddhist perspective on creativity has permeated most Oriental cultures—in but differing degrees—with the result that, prior to the disasters imported by the violent wars of the West, the despair and futility associated with Western thought in the past century have never taken root in these traditions. An utterly elusive Buddhist flavor pervades their lives. Except as one has felt the atmosphere of these people by extended immersion in their culture, statements such as the following by John M. Koller may seem like gross exaggeration:

> In the twenty-five hundred years since its beginnings, Buddhism has spread throughout Asia and has made its way even to the other continents, claiming over four hundred million followers at the present time. During this time no wars have been fought and no blood shed in the propagation of the teaching. Violence is absolutely contrary to the teachings and practice of Buddhism. It is a common conviction of Buddhists everywhere that anger and violence only provoke more of the same, and that anger and violence are only appeased and removed by kindness and compassion. The compassion demonstrated by Gautama as he traveled around the countryside teaching the causes and cessation of suffering has permeated all of Buddhism. As a result of the Buddhist emphasis on self-discipline and self-purification, it is common practice for Buddhists everywhere to concentrate on emptying themselves of everything impure and conducive to suffering. The aim is to enable a person to participate directly in reality without the intermediaries of false selves, desires, and ambitions estranging him from reality. The mark of these meditative practices in Buddhist lands is a calm peacefulness that characterizes the majority of the people.[32]

Such meditative practices constitute the major foundation of the Buddhist perspective. Buddhism is a powerful method

32. John M. Koller, *Oriental Philosophies*, pp. 192–193.

of magnification with which to bring into sharpened focus those inveterate tendencies men and women display for seeking their identity and security in the form, rather than in the creativity that brings all forms into existence. Most people are perceived in Buddhism as being fixated with the finite and neglectful of the unlimited connectedness between entities and their living matrix. The hypnotic grip of mental habits, of parochial patterns and social convention, serve as great barriers to understanding. As John Wheeler has recently remarked, "The universe is far stranger and more beautiful than we realize, and also far more simple. But we have no hope of seeing how simple it is until we first recognize how strange it is. The search for standards of intelligibility which are as unparochial as possible, which can be appreciated by the widest possible range of possible beings, and not merely by human beings from a particular culture, is a fundamental feature of the development of knowledge."[33] The more *intelligible* things become, the more unfamiliar and beautiful they are destined to be.

Buddhism constitutes one of the major resources, therefore, in the struggle of the contemporary world to free itself from the culture-bound astigmatisms of the past. Only through long and undistracted meditation is it possible to banish the continuing dialogue of outmoded notions usually found at the core of conscious awareness. Eventually, however, the victory is won, and a sustained appreciation becomes possible for the momentary nows that run like myriads of waves appearing and subsiding in the organic wholeness of things. Through meditation one breaks the grip of the goals and goods that take charge of the unrepeatable now. Success in such endeavor frees one from what is merely repetitive, mechanical, stereotyped, and compulsive. Failure to make such penetration accounts for the worst suffering of this world. It is for reasons such as these that men and women frequently spend

33. Quoted in Nicholas Maxwell, "The Rationality of Scientific Discovery," pp. 270–271.

as much as half of their annual vacations at one of the numerous meditation centers in Buddhist lands, seeking victory over their daily habit-ridden routine in government offices and commercial affairs. Meditation, indeed, can become so satisfying in this respect that it may divert a Buddhist political leader like U Nu from giving adequate attention to affairs of state, a complaint lodged against U Nu when he lost control to his rival, General Ne Win, in the coup d'etat in Rangoon of February 1962.

Under the influence of Buddhism, people of South Asia harbor an uncanny suspicion of the social sources of their fixations. Research has uncovered a predisposition "to be wary of the vested interests, the ambitions, and the presumptions of authority of man over man that are the inescapable accompaniments of human organizations."[34] Dominant social institutions are perceived as self-serving, in education, public health, religion, and all of the control systems in which non-Buddhist populations display more confident trust. It is unthinkable to many citizens of the United States that political action is not their best available means for improving the quality of life. From a Buddhist perspective, on the contrary, political structures reflect the quality that people are capable of achieving in their own experience, one individual at a time. In the only society we know anything about, Bhikkhu Nanananda in a recent Sri Lanka publication comments, "men and women perch complacently on their cozy conceptual superstructures regarding the world." Nanananda forcefully argues that "the entire conceptual structure has to leave; even those concepts that have rendered unto us the greatest assistance in our spiritual endeavor have to make their bow."[35] In fact, people in Buddhist communities are warned repeatedly against taking any concept, even a concept of the Buddha, or of Nirvana, as the definitive principle of their lives. The same is to be said of inflexible institutional form. Buddhism does not offer man

34. W. Howard Wriggins, *Ceylon*, p. 190.
35. Bhikkhu Nanananda, *Concept and Reality in Early Buddhist Thought*, pp. 75, 40.

the vision of a new society in which he will be free; freedom cannot become a social fact until the battle has been won in the white light of creative solitude within. Regardless of their promise, programs for the reorganization of human institutions cannot but express the discord of the inner man.

Humankind has yet to create forms of social existence that reinforce vivid awareness of the creativity that has been the preoccupation of Buddhists over the years. Social institutions have power of survival long after conditions calling them into being have disappeared. Institutions may well harbor incurable propensities that smother and choke what Nāgārjuna calls "the claws of wisdom" and "the living thirst" with which everything begins. We possess only remnant insights as to why the only linguistic and cultural systems we know anything about tend overwhelmingly to suppress awareness of the unity in every momentary now, reproducing year after year and generation after generation the snared and tunneled existence of the suffering world.

Leading Buddhists through the centuries have always used conceptual forms to root out conflict and suffering and to penetrate into the creativity of life. As people become free from clinging and manage a degree of disengagement from their own compulsive drives, they can use concepts and even construct elaborate conceptual systems as instruments for widening and vivifying awareness. The general thrust of Buddhism, therefore, is not against reason; it is only against culture-encapsulated and ego-centered reason, the dominant theoretical superstructures of the modern world. In fact, of the man whose influence in Buddhism compares favorably with the impact of Plato in the West, recent Buddhist scholarship affirms that "without reason guiding one's inquiry, one cannot understand anything. Nāgārjuna's philosophy cannot be characterized as a thorough-going program of invalidating conceptual thought."[36]

Creative theorizing, according to Buddhism, can lead beyond all anthropomorphic perspectives and penetrate to the

36. R. Puligandla and K. Puhakka, "Nāgārjuna and Māyā," p. 71.

creativity which is the universal principle of causation. "Understanding", as Hartshorne has shown, "must justify itself by enriching the present. Understanding should mean a higher mode of existence. Something is wrong if understanding robs us of peace in the present, only so that we may, given luck, prolong our anxious existence into old age."[37] It is therefore a perverse sort of rationality that would consider Buddhism a philosophy of unreason. The proper role of reason, Alexander Pope to the contrary, is not the study of mankind but the promotion of all that is creative in the living world, particularly in the expanding matrix of the biosphere at large.

Buddhism is humanity's first systematic attempt to free itself from what Freud called the tyranny of the superego, and from what Wittgenstein called the tyranny of language. Buddhists have never tried to control life in themselves and others under the dictates of an existing form of understanding, regardless of how hallowed its source. No one can miss the Buddhist emphasis that the "claws of wisdom" are used properly to burst the established order of ignorance and greed.

This Buddhist orientation to the deeper and vaster world of which everyone has an occasional surmise accounts for the fact that the power of the Buddhist perspective always depends, not upon its being intellectually explained and understood, but upon its being practiced "with diligence," as the Buddha stressed in his last words, far from the printed page. Buddhism is not fundamentally another system of thought; it is a way of feeling that which holds the universe together, experiencing in the fleeting now the creativity that sustains a world. The aim of any and all reflection and study for the Buddhist is to awaken to the creative rhythm in the flow of life itself. Enlightenment is not an intellectual condition but an experience of freedom from habit-ridden schedules and routine, an awakening to the ultimate momentum of life. Enlightenment points to the fact that an individual's momentary nows are centered in the zone of silence at the point where novel forms of togetherness are flowing forth out of the foun-

37. Charles Hartshorne, *The Logic of Perfection*, p. 240.

dations of the world. It is for this reason that Buddhists are encouraged "to set free the sense of the real from its moorings in abstractions."[38]

Concepts emerge in this struggle for freedom; they emerge from the depths beneath or beyond the range of conscious awareness, bearing witness to the creativity that is in man "as a living thirst to regain the dynamic, organic relatedness in which richness of life consists," as another student of Nāgārjuna has recently written.[39] The idea of Nirvana, perhaps the surpassing example of concepts functioning in this way, refers to the energizing factor within the plastic, convention-bound, ego-dominated environment. Buddhism may be called humankind's most persistent thrust toward fuller and freer participation in the creativity incarnate in the passage of temporal fact.

The major modern philosopher of Japan, Kitarō Nishida, attests, in a Buddhist vein, that "the merely conceptual is not the real; the world of actuality is the world of self-creation, a creative world which goes on forming itself; we are all creative elements of a creative world. In contradistinction to Western culture which considers form as existence and formation as good, the urge to see the form of the formless, and hear the sound of the soundless lies at the foundation of Eastern culture."[40] Nishida is speaking here of the conjunctive fullness that is deepest and nearest in the connectedness of life. The urge to be open to this concrete fullness of existence finds its most powerful and explicit expression in the Buddhist tradition.

What has kept the central conception of Buddhism viable and relevant across twenty-five centuries, however, is not the

38. K. Venkata Ramanan, *Nāgārjuna's Philosophy*, pp. 329–330.
39. Ibid., p. 38.
40. Kitarō Nishida, *Fundamental Problems of Philosophy*, pp. 45ff., 249, 252; idem, "The Problem of Japanese Culture," pp. 867ff.; and idem, *A Study of Good*, p. 211. Like Whitehead's "feeling," and Peirce's "quality" (his category of Firstness), Nishida's "pure experience" is prior to any distinctions whatsoever, including the inference of a self having the experience.

logical arguments offered in its behalf as much as this: no man or woman is so poor that he or she does not feel echoing from the deeps of experience on occasion the need and thirst to become more fully alive. As Hartshorne affirms: "We were made to be participants in creation, or, as Jules Lequier and Gustav Fechner believe, it is our destiny to be creators of ourselves."[41]

The ultimate source of one's identity, therefore, is found in casting oneself as fully as possible into the keeping of the creativity that sustains the world, the creativity that is forever unifying and enriching the diverse, divisive, and disparate nature of things. The capacity to focus upon the passing moment where life responds vividly and joyously to life is something with which the human order has a natural destiny and career.

PARALLEL DEVELOPMENTS

Parallel Developments: A Comparative History of Ideas, a recent book by Hajime Nakamura, presents similar discoveries occurring over the centuries in East and West, apart from any apparent influence of either tradition upon the other.[42] Examples of just such discoveries, recent breakthroughs in two areas of modern science bear impressively upon the Buddhist concept of relational origination. One such parallel development, discussed later in this chapter, has appeared in the field of high energy physics. The major models of theoretical physics—and this is the thesis of Fritjof Capra's book, *The Tao of Physics*—involve philosophical conceptions which are in striking agreement with those found in the Buddhist tradition. The other parallel development is now occurring on the frontiers of research into the nature of human health.

The medical model that has dominated modern medicine and

41. Hartshorne, *Creative Synthesis*, pp. xi, 277; idem, *The Logic of Perfection*, p. 259.
42. See Hajime Nakamura, *Parallel Developments*.

agencies of public health for centuries is presently being rejected in favor of a new holistic concept of health, one that incorporates all sciences of the contemporary world—physical, biological, and social. The new concept is bringing these disciplines together, as in the "Congress of the International College of Psychosomatic Medicine" whose fourth annual meeting was held in September, 1977, at Kyoto, Japan. The Congress was designed "to explore the meaning of the whole person."

Research pooled in the Kyoto meeting served to reinforce the persuasion that health cannot be understood as the absence of disease. All organs may be functioning in optimum capacity, behavior may be following conventional guidelines of what is acceptable, and no virus may be disturbing homeostasis; and yet the whole organism may be screaming out to the world that *something is wrong*. On this frontier of research the idea is growing that health is placed in jeopardy when the creativity of life is impaired. The measures of health are flexibility, freedom from compulsive drives, openness to life's qualitative flow, and the wish to struggle to become more vividly and widely aware. The new concept focuses attention upon the major anaesthetizing aspects of behavior—rigidity in what can be experienced, mechanization in "seeing" and "behaving," dogmatism in what is believed, active inattention to novelties in experience, and inability to accept conflict between incompatible goods as an unavoidable fact of life.

The new concept of health focuses attention upon everything that impairs the capacity for experiencing one's own experience, feeling the concrete fullness of existence in its qualitative flow where men and women are memorably and vitally alive. There is an emphasis upon life being centered in immediate unbroken contact with the organic relatedness of things. In hundreds of journals and books the following type of remark grows ever more frequent: "Mankind is increasingly aware of the prison it has built for itself, and individuals want to be freed from what they are made to swallow by their environment. Because of this, man's metaphysical drive is leading him in the direction of expression, liberation, revelation from within."[43] In lectures at Harvard University, Lawrence Kubie stated that "any moment of behavior is neurotic if the processes that set it in motion predetermine its automatic repetition."[44] Habit-ridden behavior is abnormal, and it can be dangerous, because it chokes off the unlimited expansion of awareness that enables men and women to cope with their problems.

People are beginning to realize that their worst problems are the ones other people are institutionalized for having. Mental patients suffer from most of the same disabilities that "normal" people have, except in a more or less aggravated degree. Both groups are institutionalized, but only one is behind visible walls. This insight holds the possibility of a self-sustaining chain reaction awakening men and women to the creativity at the center of their lives which, in the Buddhist concept of relational origination, is the sun around which their species is able in freedom to revolve.

The holistic view of health as a positive state of personal fulfillment suggests in some ways the ideal of the *Bodhisattva*, who symbolizes the optimal creativity or relational power forever synthesizing in his own compassionate experience the shared experience of all. The *Bodhisattva* has attained that state of fullness or completeness in which preceding degrees of experiential togetherness are surpassed forevermore.

As was previously suggested, the field of high energy physics is another area of parallel development between East and West. The Buddhist view that reality is a process of relational origination, or creative synthesis, finds positive reinforcement in the work of a long line of distinguished scientists— Einstein, Werner Heisenberg, Max Planck, Ernest Rutherford, Niels Bohr, Max Born, Leo Szilard, Enrico Fermi, Robert Oppenheimer, Arthur Compton—all of whom prepared the way for particle physics and the new views now emerging of the subatomic world. Utilizing the most expensive and ingenious technology ever imagined, at such centers as the Fermi

43. Claudio Naranjo and Robert E. Ornstein, *On the Psychology of Meditation*, p. 230.
44. Lawrence S. Kubie, *Neurotic Distortions of the Creative Process*, p. 97.

National Laboratory in Batavia, Illinois, and the Centre Européen de Recherches Nucléaires (CERN) in Geneva, Switzerland, the objects and substances of the everyday world turn out to be parts of an intrinsically dynamic universe in which the physicist must be reconceived as a participant rather than an independent observer. Quanta of energy (bundles of energy considered as particles), always in a state of motion and change, are part of an interrelated infinite variety of forms in which nothing has *svabhāva* ("self-established nature"). Everything and everyone are processes related in a cosmic web that is alive.

A statement by Henry Stapp will serve as an illustration of this central point:

> One finds in the realm of experience essentially the same type of structure that one finds in the realm of elementary-particle physics, namely a web structure, the smallest elements of which always reach out to other things and find their meaning and ground of being in these other things. Since this same type of structure is suitable both in the realm of mind and in the realm of matter, one is led to adopt it as the basis of an over-all world view.
>
> An experience is an integral part of some web of experience. Experiences cannot be analyzed into ultimate unanalyzable entities. The component parts invariably reach out to things outside themselves. To isolate an experience from its references is to destroy its essence. In short, experiences must be viewed as parts of webs, whose parts are not defined except through their connections to the whole.[45]

These observations, Stapp goes on to say, are "definitely incompatible with the idea that the actual things of nature reside in the space-time continuum of classical physics." The most commonly observed objection to the classical mechanistic model is that it contributes no adequate understanding of the connection of the mechanical quantities to experience. "If one goes outside the mechanistic framework," Stapp explains, "then one can view the measurement and its result, not in terms of con-

45. Henry Peirce Stapp, "S-Matrix Interpretation of Quantum Theory," p. 1319.

cretely existing space-time structures, but rather in terms of webs of relations. The description of the measurement and its result is expressed in terms of words. These words are parts of an enveloping web of words called language. This web derives its meaning from the webs of experience into which it is woven."[46]

The Buddhist perspective of relational origination, or creative synthesis, in a continuity of momentary nows, each inheriting the "ripening fruit" of the past, contains the basic elements of the world view now emerging, as Capra seeks to show in his book devoted to the similarities involved. "The two basic themes of this conception," Capra writes, "are the unity and interrelation of all phenomena and the intrinsically dynamic nature of the universe. The further we penetrate into the sub-microscopic world, the more we shall realize how the modern physicist has come to see the world as a system of inseparable, interacting and ever-moving components with man being an integral part of the system."[47] Each must work out his salvation with diligence as a participant in this complicated web of existence.

Subtle influences link all parts of the world, and to become more fully aware of the organic wholeness presupposes not only an intellectual act but an involvement on the part of the whole person.

The Eastern view of the world [Capra continues] is 'organic'. All things and events perceived by the senses are interrelated, connected, and are but different aspects or manifestations of the same ultimate reality. Our tendency to divide the perceived world into individual and separate things and to experience ourselves as isolated egos in this world is seen as an illusion which comes from our measuring and categorizing mentality. It is called *avidyā*, or ignorance, in Buddhist philosophy and is seen as the state of a disturbed mind which has to be overcome.[48]

46. Ibid., p. 1320; Ibid. pp. 1318–1319. "The world is either fundamentally lawless or fundamentally inseparable" (p. 1308).
47. Fritjof Capra, *The Tao of Physics*, p. 25.
48. Ibid., pp. 23–24.

A self-identical self is not necessary for the experiences of the passing moment to be bound together, for they are already together in the flow, preserved as the unique, concrete enjoyers or sufferers of existence in the one thread of everlasting identity pervasive of all space and time. This is the view presently emerging out of areas of modern science which appear to have nothing to do with one another—the holistic concept of health emerging on the frontiers of a new socially oriented and philosophically curious psychosomatic medicine, and the experience of the wholeness of nature in a field of interrelated forms now communicated to us by the high-energy physicist of our time.

These new developments from widely separated areas of modern science are not, of course, as entirely novel as they seem, for they have been anticipated by hundreds of penetrating minds of both East and West. In the case of the East, the insights are part of the orientation long dominant in Buddhist lands. In the case of the West, however, they constitute a largely submerged orientation that began with Heraclitus and then suffered from almost total neglect until comparatively recent times when it was resurrected in the writings of Ernst Heinrich Haeckel, Gustav Theodor Fechner, Henri Bergson, Samuel Alexander, Charles Sanders Peirce, William James, John Dewey, Alfred North Whitehead, and the only major American philosopher with wide reading in the Buddhist tradition, Charles Hartshorne.

Parallel developments from widely separated areas of inquiry embody together a momentum driving us into a new orientation of life, where the fragmentation of culture-bound individuals will have been healed and overcome. Creativity is the principle of all becoming, encountered in experiences to which no one but the individual involved can give the final touch. The Buddhist denial of any self-established entity, a denial which, if taken seriously, suggests the ignorance of all tendency to cling, leads in its vision of "relational origination" to what Capra calls "a cultural revolution in the true sense of the word."

Most of today's physicists [Capra further writes] do not seem to realize the philosophical, cultural and spiritual implications of their theories. Many of them actively support a society which is still based on the mechanistic, fragmented world view, without seeing that science points beyond such a view, towards a oneness of the universe which includes not only our natural environment but also our fellow human beings. I believe that the world view implied by modern physics is inconsistent with our present society, which does not reflect the harmonious interrelatedness we observe in nature. To achieve such a state of dynamic balance, a radically different social and economic structure will be needed: a cultural revolution in the true sense of the word. The survival of our whole civilization may depend on whether we can bring about such a change.[49]

The thrill of life, according to the Buddhist perspective, is found in the living itself. Individuals discover that the qualities with which life is pregnant constitute their own reward. A certain opaqueness is all that prevents anyone from perceiving that reality is of momentary experiences, not of things or egos; that uncertainty and risk are the accompaniment of every fleeting now; that the present can only be poisoned and rendered more uncertain still by postponing life into an indefinite future, or in other ways seeking to have life in some sense without really having it at all. For the moment, the choice is ours. Working in the medium of the passing now, we are the artists of our lives. Attending ever more fully to the vivid qualities of our experience, we become more aware and awake and capable of the affirmation of worth that is the vitality of life itself.

For twenty-five centuries, Buddhism has advanced this central conception and distinguished itself in its orientation to a world governed neither by an autonomous Being nor by blind chance, but "by the law of spiritual and material interrelatedness which is neither simple causality nor metaphysical determinism, but the law of Dependent Origination (*pratītya-samutpāda*); it is the idea that nothing exists in itself or by

49. Ibid., pp. 307–308.

itself as a separate unit, but is dependent on a variety of conditions and related to everything else in the world."[50] The *Mūlamadhyamakakārikā* opens with the stunning verse:

> Without destruction and without origination,
> Without being cut off and without being eternal,
> Neither being one thing, nor different things,
> Neither coming nor going,
> He who can thus teach the Dependent Origination,
> The blissful coming to rest of all illusory unfoldment,
> Before Him, the Enlightened One, the best of teachers,
> I reverently bow down.[51]

And from the Middle Kingdom across the Himalayas centuries later the *Platform Sutra* continues:

> If within and without you are not deluded then you are apart from duality. If on the outside you are deluded you cling to form; if on the inside you are deluded you cling to emptiness. If within form you are apart from form and within emptiness you are separated from emptiness, then within and without you are not deluded.[52]

From the outset, this is the Dharma that has been in the world.[53] Like the flower wedded to the sun, all existences and phenomena constitute an interrelated creative One.

50. P. V. Bapat, ed., *2500 Years of Buddhism*, p. 326.
51. Ibid., p. 327.
52. Philip B. Yampolsky, trans., *The Platform Sutra of the Sixth Patriarch*, p. 166.
53. Ibid., p. 161.

4

⌇⌇⌇⌇⌇⌇⌇⌇⌇⌇⌇⌇⌇⌇⌇⌇⌇⌇⌇⌇⌇⌇⌇⌇⌇⌇⌇⌇⌇⌇⌇⌇

Nirvana: The Aesthetic Center of Life

Nirvana, O King, is unproducible, and no cause for its origin has been declared. And why? Because Nirvana is not put together of any qualities. It is uncompounded, not made of anything. Of Nirvana, O King, it cannot be said that it has been produced, or not produced, or that it can be produced, that it has past or future or present, that it is perceptible by the eye or the ear or the nose or the tongue or by the sense of touch. Nirvana exists, O King. And it is perceptible to the mind. By means of his pure heart, refined and straight, free from the obstacles, free from low cravings, that disciple of the Noble One who has fully attained can see Nirvana.

Milindapañha
(Questions of King Milinda)

THE WHOLE PURPOSE of the generalizing insights we pursue in Buddhist philosophy is to open our experience to more of the aesthetic richness flowing deep in the inarticulate rhythms of our bodies, where immense quantities of experience are stored from ages past. In its concept of Nirvana, Buddhism sends a shaft of light into those depths where the flow of quality after long and strenuous meditation is apprehended in ways freed from psychosomatic and cultural designs, freed from all that is repetitive, mechanical, stereotyped, and compulsive in our lives.

The whole nisus of our being is toward the fullness of quality communicating its distinctive power with a richness no glorified image or collective living can ever deliver. The greatest hunger or thirst for which we live is for direct experience of the vividness and richness of life itself, purified of the distortions of conscious intentions and independent of anything we can think or do.

This is the universal hunger to which all human cultures are unresponsive, for reasons that become obvious the more closely they are examined. The basic motivation in every compassionate man or woman is for the increasing depth and intensification of quality that makes *each fugitive moment unique forever*. Beyond the ways in which individuals, down to their very glands and nervous systems are rendered responsive by cultural conditioning to certain meanings and objectives, there is the undifferentiated, unitary, fundamental quality of Nirvana, redeeming life from meaninglessness and despair. In his concept of Nirvana, the Buddha paid his highest honor to humankind.

In Nirvana an individual is free at last—"in the clearing," as Heidegger puts it—free to open himself to the aesthetic foundations of the world. From the very beginning nothing has been kept from us, all that we wished to see has been there all the time before us, it was only ourselves that closed the door. Nirvana is the consummatory experience of being released from the forced and driven state of personal and social directives. It is life's deepest unconscious aim to experience this qualitative fullness in the *now*.

The more highly developed the human mind becomes, the greater is its capacity for Nirvana. Nirvana is not a vision, mystical or otherwise; it is a transformation of the individual through the illumination of life whereby all the rich qualities *underlying* one's discriminations come into the foreground of awareness. Rigid stereotyped responses once commanding attention retire into the background of the human cave, leaving fully and freely operative the total capacity of the organism for experiencing the concrete undifferentiated flow of quality out of the foundations of the world.

Experience for everyone begins, as Charles Sanders Peirce says, with a feeling of quality, "perfectly simple and irrespective of anything else, undivided, without parts, the moment as it is in its singleness, without regard to its relations whether to its own elements or to anything else."[1] Awareness of this moment of quality is first in one's experience, whatever its import may be, allowing no inference concerning its eventual outcome,[2] and, as all Buddhists have insisted, permitting no inference regarding an ego or substantial self. The only world-renowned philosopher of science in the American tradition, Peirce confirms the Buddhist perspective that the self, along with similar general ideas, is only inferred; intellect is rooted in feeling. This rootedness of the intellect is the great insight achieved by Hume and developed into an ontology by Whitehead. General ideas, Peirce also argued, are themselves "living feelings spread out."[3]

Nirvana therefore implies an invitation to grow from our deepest underground roots, absorbing from these roots the power to reflect in our behavior the organic nature of the world, and thus becoming too strong to need others upon whom we may lean, and too strong to need authoritarian figures whom we may follow in the mass movements of the present world.

Nirvana thus makes possible a more fully evolved person, one capable of winning the inner struggle against unconscious wastelands, and of extending the range of a person's powers far beyond what hitherto has been imagined. Nirvana is an adventure in human fulfillment, an experience of deliverance from anxiety, disability and despair. No one who has awakened to this qualitative richness and experienced those consummatory heights of joy is ever capable of living to "stay alive," or to measure life by length of years.

The supreme Buddhist criterion of a humane social order is found in the qualitative richness of the experience of its members. Almost alone among the philosophies of humanity, Buddhism says that joy is the natural condition of a human's life. Theoretically, there is no reason why social agencies might not be designed to awaken, rather than deaden, the thirst individuals have by nature for enhancing the qualitative full-

1. *Collected Papers of Charles Sanders Peirce*, vol. 7, pars. 538–540.
2. Ibid., vol. 5, par. 462.
3. Ibid., vol. 6, par. 143.

ness of the moment. In its early records, as Nanananda has shown, Buddhism emphasizes that "what is void as to concepts is *not* devoid of happiness." On the contrary, when proper conditions are provided, *"then there will be joy and happiness, and peace, and in continual mindfulness and self-mastery, one will dwell at ease."*[4] Working with early sources accessible to him in Sri Lanka, Jayatilleke found that "it is of the nature of things that delight arises in a joyful person; a person who is joyful need not determine in his mind that delight should arise in him. *It is in the nature of things (dhammatā) that* joy arises in a person who lacks remorse."[5] Out of the 121 classes of consciousness intricately mapped and analyzed in early Buddhist psychology, Govinda affirms, "sixty-three are accompanied by joy. The more man progresses, the more radiant and joyful will be his consciousness. Happiness, indeed, may be called a characteristic of progress." Of five *jhānas* ("higher states of consciousness"), joy is left behind only in the highest two.[6]

Buddhism is thus the celebration of the joy of living, the joy being the natural expression or "voice" of the vivid quality and heightened awareness flowing in those original centers of experience where life is becoming ever more fully a work of art. To the extent that we struggle free from pseudoidentities (i.e. those that are socially imposed and self-centered), and experience what in present-centered moments we are *truly experiencing*, remorse over the past and the postponement of life into an indefinite future are banished completely, simply by incorporating into the passing moment that unity, wholeness, balance, honesty, depth, proportion and heightened vitality that distinguish every great work of art. This is why great works of art have had a more lasting impact upon humanity than the most powerful empires of the past. The power of art resembles the power of Buddhist meditation; it loosens the flow of quality from behind the frontier where precision

4. Bhikkhu Nanananda, *Concept and Reality in Early Buddhist Thought*, pp. 75, 98.

5. K. N. Jayatilleke, *Early Buddhist Theory of Knowledge*, p. 448.

6. Lama Anagarika Govinda, *The Psychological Attitude of Early Buddhist Philosophy*, pp. 63, 86.

of consciousness fails. "In art," as Whitehead states, "the finite consciousness of mankind is appropriating as its own the infinite fecundity of nature."[7]

Bergson may have been the first philosopher in Europe to catch this central insight independently of direct influence from Buddhist writings. "In the depths of our experience," the Sorbonne professor writes, "at the point where we feel ourselves most intimately within our own life," the joy of burgeoning quality swells unceasingly "with a present that is absolutely new." Bergson takes special pains to distinguish this joy from the pleasure of traditional hedonism and its reformulation in the British Utilitarian school. "Pleasure," he writes, "is only a contrivance devised by nature to obtain for the creature the preservation of its life; it does not indicate the direction in which life is thrusting. But joy always announces that life has gained ground. All great joy has a triumphant note."[8]

Lancelot Whyte, if one may judge from posthumous publications, probably penetrated into this organic nature of joy more deeply than anyone in the discipline of modern physics. "Joy," he believes, "is an unsought state of grace in which life is enhanced and the imagination is surpassed, the awareness of being vividly alive." Continuing, he says,

This capacity for joy is given to man in his heredity, and only a dissociated culture can take it away. Persistent suffering cannot be borne without moments of joy. At the root lies this principle: man should not die without having lived, without having experienced enough joy to bring him peace when the end is near. The values which follow from joy are not moral, but aesthetic: openness to experience; respect for the uniqueness of the individual; tolerance toward variety; unification of emotion, idea, and action; immediacy and spontaneity in experience and action. It is this aesthetic relief which takes the sting from death, and the more joy he has experienced in life, the easier he can remain serene amid disaster.[9]

7. Alfred North Whitehead, *Adventures of Ideas*, pp. 350–351.
8. Henri Bergson, *Creative Evolution*, pp. 199–200. See also Bergson, *Mind-Energy*, pp. 29–30.
9. Lancelot Law Whyte, *The Universe of Experience*, pp. 98–100.

The more actualized the native capacities for joy, Whyte continues, the more man regains his sense of direction in the contemporary world. "Today," he says, "man is pathological in a virulent degree," but there is now "a movement within the human psyche sensing that *organic nature is on our side*, bringing to fruition a new awareness born of insights long before us which culminate and suddenly crystallize in an organic and aesthetic metamorphosis of life."[10] Whyte believed that this metamorphosis may now occur in a single generation, so broad and profound are the insights into the aesthetic foundations burgeoning in the present world. A Buddhist could hardly have been expected to write such words more forcibly out of a lifetime in the physical and biological sciences. Whyte meets the specifications of Richard Lannoy's study of Indian culture, in which Lannoy comments that "some of the most advanced Western thinking of our day is devoted to the problem of reconciling the aesthetic with the scientific, while overcoming the disastrous effects of having allowed bourgeois aesthetic culture to have become implicated in modern fascism. There is every hope that India may play a positive role in this reconciliation."[11]

Twenty-five centuries ago the Buddha proposed this norm for human experience: life undergoes endless suffering and degenerates when enclosed within the deadening influence and pressures of habit-ridden social conformity. Nature is lavish in its aesthetic richness, and, as Govinda affirms, "the longer we can abstain from seeing things habitually, the more profoundly we shall be conscious of their true nature, which goes beyond concepts and definitions. Habit kills intuition, because it prevents living experience."[12] Beyond the breakdown, Govinda teaches, of individuals and nations, beyond the frustration of human hopes, beyond the relentless sweep of time and destructiveness which ruin every other ground upon which one may take one's stand, there is the fullness of the aesthetic

10. Ibid., pp. 100–103.
11. Richard Lannoy, *The Speaking Tree*, p. 79.
12. Lama Anagarika Govinda, *Creative Meditation and Multi-Dimensional Consciousness*, p. 157.

center of life, the flow of unstructured quality, unlimited in its intensification and stimulation of each moment in even the common and ordinary affairs of life, providing that one is able to penetrate the confinements of language and cultural pattern. One of the Buddhist monks of Rangoon taught me a *mettā* meditation that has grown through the years:

> May he (she, it, they) be well and happy,
> May he (she, it, they) cope creatively with suffering,
> Experiencing forever the flow of quality
> Out of the living foundations of the world.

It is a good illustration of the practical emphasis in the Buddha's teaching. Repeated for periods of one-half hour duration each day, the meditation has the power to redeem the inner life from meaninglessness and despair, but only because it serves to awaken the deepest responsiveness of the human organism to the infinitely rich quality, the aesthetic fullness no words can really convey. The world is this rich fullness of quality, hidden and abandoned beneath the distractions of the day.

Apart from this awakening to the unstructured aesthetic continuum deep in every human heart,[13] the human adventure is implicated in some aboriginal calamity; it is out of step with the rhythm of existence. However, "by virtue of Nirvana," as Inada writes, "there is that sense of power, vitality, quality, freedom, and self-active creativity with which everything begins."[14] It is important to stress that this qualitative fullness is in every passing moment. Nirvana is *now* forevermore, not

13. Burmese intellectuals like U Khin Maung Win, my guide during 1961–1962 research year at the International Institute for Advanced Buddhistic Studies, found Northrop's phrase, "undifferentiated aesthetic continuum," a practical English equivalent for Nirvana. See F. S. C. Northrop, *The Meeting of East and West*, pp. 376, 399, 435, 472–475.
14. Kenneth K. Inada, Comments on "Creativity in the Buddhist Perspective." Inada was kind enough to send me a typescript of his comments on my "Creativity in the Buddhist Perspective," a paper read April 29, 1976 at a philosophy meeting in New Orleans, and later published (see Nolan Pliny Jacobson, "Creativity in the Buddhist Perspective"). The sentence commented upon is on page 53: *"The reality of experience is marked by the sense*

reproducing what has been, nor bringing creation to a consummatory final end. Nirvana represents the organic connection of every passing moment and every single being with all that exists and is alive. Life means giving and taking, breathing in and breathing out, taking possession of nothing, and responding on the nonverbal and noncultural level to everything and everyone we touch. "The complete and direct awareness of the unique moment in the infinity of time and space and the eternity of life," Govinda stresses, "is the highest achievement of meditation, which ultimately means the realization of solidarity with all living beings." Furthermore, "we do not suffer because everything is impermanent, but because we cling to impermanent things. If we did not cling to them, we should not mind their impermanence."[15] Buddhism develops a way of life which orients men and women to the deepest level of existence where the flow of quality continuously awakens them from the humdrum and fills them with the wonder of being alive.

It is quality of which everything is made, and quality means energy to human experience; a weak life experiences little qualitative flow in the fugitive moments of a day, as any physician will confirm. Nirvana, then, is "the energizing factor within the mundane nature of things, i.e. within the so-called conventionally constructed or conditioned realm which becomes the framework from which ordinary empirical transactions take place," as Inada states. This "energizing factor," he continues, "is Nirvana." Furthermore, "Nirvana, as the ultimate goal and aim of all Buddhists, can be realized with all the empirical residues remaining; that is to say, in the here and now, within the nature of our own faculties and endowments, when all lusting and attachments to the elements which hamper the free and rich flow in existence have been resolved."[16]

---

of quality and power with which it begins." Inada's sentence goes beyond my own in ways relevant to the present chapter.

15. Govinda, *Creative Meditation*, pp. 209–210, 185.

16. Inada, Comments on "Creativity," pp. 1–2. Inada uses the Sanskrit term *upadhiśeṣa-nirvāṇa*.

The concreteness and particularity of this aesthetic foundation have been stressed in all the Buddhist writings of the past. "Suffering of life does not prompt one to abandon life," Nāgārjuna is said to have written. "It is one's mission to attain to the Highest Good, a good that is non-exclusive. It is a comprehensive attitude where one takes interest in every little thing without being confined anywhere, for here one is aware of the place and function of everything, as well as of its ultimate meaning."[17]

In such fulfillment at the center of solitariness in one's life, "everyone and everything," as Masao Abe writes, "is enriched without eliminating its differentiation. This is the living structure of Nirvana, the free flow of living quality with no attachment to arrest the flow." Masao Abe complains, moreover, that "instead of obscuring or obliterating the differentiation of everyone and everything"—as Abe argues Buddhism has so often been falsely translated and understood—"individuality is fulfilled in Nirvana, everyone and everything becoming increasingly capable of synthesizing and assimilating qualities that are pregnant in all the rest. Each then becomes capable of having that particular effect which in all the universe no other could produce."[18]

The awareness and the aesthetic fullness of Nirvana are one; this is why the attainment of Nirvana is the consummatory experience of life. Despite its being smothered by compulsions, preoccupations, and distractions, some measure of this unity dwells naturally in every heart. It would be tempting for Buddhists to think of Nirvana as being communicable from master to disciple; but it would be too easy to listen, too easy to teach. What makes a life-struggle out of the quest for Nirvana is the extreme difficulty of discovering the indwell-

17. K. Venkata Ramanan, *Nāgārjuna's Philosophy*, pp. 329–330. In this work, now considered a later synthesis of his major ideas, Nāgārjuna claims that by penetrating the fragmentary and compulsive character, and by penetrating our mooring in abstractions, we are restored to our original organic confidence in creation.

18. Masao Abe, Rev. of *Christianity and the Encounter of the World Religions*, by Paul Tillich, p. 114. Cf. Alfred North Whitehead, *Modes of Thought*, p. 119.

ing secret of one's own life. What is closest remains the most difficult to perceive. "Awakening and self-realization and seeing into one's own being—these," Suzuki remarks, "are all synonymous—they are what is meant by Satori."[19] It needs no further emphasis: Nirvana is a personal experience, and not a merging of the empirical individual in some extraterrestrial realm, such as the "upper world" of a "mystical geography" resorted to by J. N. Findlay and others.[20]

It should be emphasized that Buddhism is one of the most thoroughgoing naturalistic disciplines the world has ever witnessed, though, as Inada observes, "it is unappreciated in this light for the most part." In opposing the esoteric tendencies of some scholars, Jean Filliozat stresses the fact that the goal of Buddhist meditation "is not 'ecstasy' as surmized by many scholars trying to find in European religious mysticism an equivalent for that actually pure psychological notion. It is by no means a raptus of the soul outside the body. On the contrary, it is a masterful domination of the entire psychological and physiological human forces, a control of all the episodical manifestations affecting the self." The same naturalistic emphasis was found by Michael Ames during field work in Sri Lanka: "Buddhists claim their philosophy does not rest upon mystical revelations but upon precise and verifiable laws discovered by the Buddha, all of which are capable of verification, so it is argued, through the development of the mind."[21]

Nirvana is the eternal greatness incarnate in the passage of temporal fact. It is the tenderness of life itself amid the senseless brutalities of this world. This "eternal joy," as Buddhists describe it, is realized with the extinction of all attitudes of servility, exploitation, compulsive striving. Having

19. Daisetz Teitaro Suzuki, *Zen and Japanese Culture*, p. 435. Buddhist monks, like Bhikkhu Paññadipa, made the same point as a regular emphasis: "The real meaning or sense of Nibbana cannot be realized until one has attained it by oneself" (from mss. on Nibbana written by the Bhikkhu).

20. J. N. Findlay, *The Transcendence of the Cave*, pp. 117, 122, 139, 178.

21. Kenneth K. Inada, Abstract of "The Ultimate Ground of Buddhist Purification," p. 146; Jean Filliozat, "The Psychological Discoveries of Buddhism," p. 73; Michael E. Ames, "Religious Syncretism in Buddhist Ceylon," p. 29.

neither past, future, nor present in its unstructured, undifferentiated flow, it is that feature of the universe that enables us
to say, "There is only the eternal *now*."[22]

Nirvana is perceptible to the mind because perception in
Buddhism is not limited to sense experience and memory, but
includes all the resources of the live creature: intuition, meditation, inference, aspiration, wonder, and the feelings within
the body resulting from its immense experience in the unlimited fecundity of nature. Such depths of feeling, beyond the
frontiers of conscious awareness, are so powerful, and the capacity for responding throughout this perceptual range is so
great, that life has never stood in need of theoretical constructs and empirical forms of understanding in order to survive and flourish. The first philosophical genius of modern Japan, Kitarō Nishida, interpreted the culture-world of his
country on this Buddhist foundation, in something he called
"pure feeling" or "pure experience," where everything in art,
science, technology, or any other cultural phenomena has its
beginning. It is on this level where the world is felt first; only
later is it, perhaps, encountered and known. In Nishida's view,
all cultural patterns are ways of feeling what is actually the
case. It is "pure experience" that gives men and women the
feeling of being vitally and memorably alive. It goes without
saying that ordinary sense perception superficially overlays
this feeling of what Nishida calls the "oneness of the manyness and the manyness-of-oneness."[23]

The forms of understanding, in the legacy of Buddhist
thought, do not confront a world of sheer disorder; they are,
on the contrary, possible ways of feeling the changing world,
possible vehicles for enhancing, intensifying and harmonizing
the richness felt in the passage of temporal fact. The major

22. Narada Thera, *A Manual of Abhidhamma*, pp. 180–181. A Canadian
bhikkhu, The Venerable U Ananda Bodhi, put it this way: "At the point
where lightning strikes, there is the realization of a new nature and this is
Nibbana. This is the *now* of salvation. Nibbana, therefore, might be called
the 'Divine Ground'."

23. Kitarō Nishida, *A Study of Good*, p. 211. See also Nishida, "Affective
Feeling."

function of reason, indeed, has been to keep men and women from those forms of thought that alienate and splinter the qualitative flow. Humanity's greatest insurance against self-destruction has always resided in the inability to predetermine and commit ourselves in advance to the conceptual structures that events induce us to harbor. In a world where the creative matrix of energy is alive in us each moment, events are knowable only after they have occurred.

Conceptual structures loom before us lucid and convincing, not because they are the logical deductions of disembodied and undistracted minds, but because they are resources—as we may have discovered—for enhancing, deepening, broadening, and vivifying the qualitative richness in the passage of temporal fact. We see farther, our knowledge improves, only as we free ourselves from the distortions and illusions that impoverish the art of living. For almost the entirety of human history, these forms of understanding have been in conflict with the flow of quality streaming across the sinews and nerve-endings of humankind. Without the tacit and preconscious levels of perception, without the flow of unstructured quality in our experience communicating an immediate sense of belonging in the totality of things, human life would have lost its orientation to the momentum of life. In the intensification and stimulation of aesthetic novelty and wholeness, we intuit something of what the cosmos can and must be.

It is the shared conclusion of men and women who are oriented toward Nirvana that everyone has an inveterate tendency to cover and obscure the qualitative flow with a multitude of *reactive* feelings. The last time we could rely on our ability to feel the qualities of our incomparable lives was probably some time before we were born. Ever since then, we have been considered normal in our attitudes toward school, family, church, athletics, music, literature, business, and political affairs only as long as our behavior has conformed to the norm for a particular age and social group. People divided internally in this way have the attitudes required for not perceiving the basic irrationality of their own way of living. People like this are capable of living out the continuing destruction of the beauty, mystery, and momentum of life-fulfilling careers in themselves and others. According to the Buddha's own teaching, such people are "writhing in delusion," suffering, they know not where, from the coercions of an invasive world. It was probably reflections such as these that led the Buddha to remark that "the ocean is not large and deep enough to contain the tears which through millions of existences fill the eyes of one man."[24]

Buddhism is humankind's most persisting effort to prevent linguistic systems, institutions, bureaucracies, and political superstitions from leading men and women away from the realities of their intuited world, their present-centeredness in experiencing value in their lives. Lama Govinda, one of the leading Buddhist scholars of our day, stresses that

We live mostly in an indirect, reactive world, and only rarely do we experience actual reality and thus live in the present. Our usual reactions are habitual, due to routine. . . . To live in the present means to see everything with a perfectly pure, unprejudiced and open mind, to experience everything as profoundly as if we had never known it before. It means to retain (or to restore) the freshness and alertness of mind which is the characteristic quality of genius. Generally we live away from life, either by being occupied with the past, or by anticipating the future. Both these attitudes of the mind mean bondage.[25]

The same point is emphasized by one of our leading psychiatrists, Claudio Naranjo. Our real feelings are "covered up by the reactive feelings that take so much of our conscious attention. . . . Even if we do not want to go so far as to speak of a relative unreality of neurotic feelings, we may still accept the notion of two sets of feelings: those of the real self in us, and those of the constructs we house in our psyche—identifications, social roles, and a proud self-ideal." The kind of personal development which is interspersed today with "patches

24. Quoted in Louis de la Vallee Poussin, *The Way to Nirvana*, p. 109.
25. Govinda, *Creative Meditation*, pp. 250–251.

of intense life"—with sudden focusing upon the wonder of being alive and the preciousness of that life—this, Naranjo says, "is essentially a change in attitudes, points of view, ways of experiencing the world."[26]

Sweden's Buddhist scholar, Rune Johannson, makes the same point in his comparative study of Nirvana and the aims of psychology in the modern world. "By definition," he writes, "nibbana [Nirvana] is therefore freedom from the emotions and desires by which egoism and attachment are created: all definitions are in complete agreement on this point. This does not mean complete absence of motivation, nor passivity."[27] What it does mean is that the individual "gets in touch," "comes to his senses," and *focuses* upon the way the brain as a reducing-valve has employed a local language to produce those shared delusions and consensual realities that suffocate, embitter, and enrage. *Satipaṭṭhāna*, the form of meditation one encounters in Burma and Sri Lanka, has developed methods over the centuries which achieve this focus and which deepen one's contact with the flow of quality in one's own experience.[28] As Malalasekera once remarked, the process of "perpetual becoming" is freed through meditation and analysis from "snares that seek to direct us to outcomes predetermined in advance."[29] The more we bring into high relief the unlimited growth of quality at those centers of experience where we are deeply and memorably alive, the less we cling compulsively to linguistic, conceptual, and self-encapsulated form. Any experience of ecstasy will serve to establish this as a fact.

The major thrust of Buddhist thought, therefore, is to awaken the eventful moments of our experience to more of the fullness of existence, to make us feel more vividly and deeply the connectedness of things, and to make us perceive

26. Claudio Naranjo, *The One Quest*, pp. 74–75, 18.

27. Rune Johannson, *The Psychology of Nirvana*, p. 110.

28. See, for example, Nyānaponika Mahāthera, *The Heart of Buddhist Meditation.*

29. Gunapala Piyasena Malalasekera, "Aspects of Reality Taught by Theravāda Buddhism," p. 78.

the universe as an organic unity of all that happens. Buddhist philosophy, when accompanied by the proposed methods of meditation, has the power to liberate people from self-centered, human-centered, culture-encapsulated limits of existence. Moved by a "thirst for organic relatedness," as Nāgārjuna taught,[30] we find in the flow of this qualitative fullness an adequate directive for living. Bergson affirms that on each of the world's forms of life, particularly humanity, "nature in an immense inflorescence of unforeseeable novelty confers the absolute value of a great work of art." And we see best, hear best, and feel most vividly and clearly when we see, hear, and feel in order to extend the range and depth of our awareness of these absolutely valued forms of life, for in us there runs a creative current, drawing much from little, something from nothing, and adding, as Bergson has it, "unceasingly to whatever wealth the world contains."[31] As the *Milindapañha (Questions of King Milinda)* says, "Those who see the reality from within, by intuition, are in direct contact with Nibbāna [Nirvana]."[32]

Lives not centered in the qualitative flow, lives not oriented toward Nirvana, enact a continuing habit of raw exploitation of self and others, postponing indefinitely the aim and purpose of life. Instead of celebrating the joy and wonder of being alive in the passing now, they move through, to use Northrop's phrase, the "aesthetically breath-taking, colorful world"[33]—eyes unseeing, ears unhearing—concerned only with the *reactive* feelings acquired from the social pressures of an enveloping world. On the other hand, to place Nirvana in a positive perspective, the testimony of the exceptional penetrations of Buddhist people of the past shows that, as Nakamura writes,

through the involuntary activity of one's nature in contact with the outer world, life as we know it goes on incessantly. One who has

30. Ramanan, *Nāgārjuna's Philosophy*, p. 330.
31. Bergson, *Mind-Energy*, pp. 31–33, 29–30.
32. *The Questions of King Milinda*, p. 268.
33. F. S. C. Northrop, Foreward to *A Whiteheadian Aesthetic*, p. xxv.

attained Enlightenment is far from having dissolved into non-being; it is not he who is extinct, but the life of illusion, passions, and desires. He no longer feels himself to be conditioned by false ideas and attendant desires. Nirvana is this lasting state of happiness and peace, the island amidst the floods, the place of emancipation, un-created, tranquil, immaterial, immortal, imperishable, the further shore.[34]

Nirvana is the continuing lure, Keiji Nishitani accurately states, "to cut the threads of attachment which tie us to things of this world. The Buddhist way means an awakening in which we become aware of our original and authentic nature (our dharma-nature) and live in conformity to it. The possibility of attaining this enlightenment depends entirely upon our-selves."[35] Nirvana lures us to find levels in our minds of which we are not aware. Its irradiation from beyond the range of symbolic systems is the most profound and harmonious matrix into which every mind and heart can awaken. "This," E. R. Sarathchandra writes, "is peace; this is Nibbana."[36] Many oth-ers have thought of Nirvana as a synonym for peace. The words Whitehead has written about peace, as Inada says, could have been written by a Buddhist about Nirvana.[37]

It is a positive feeling, momentous in its coordination of values. Its first effect is the removal of stress of acquisitive feeling arising from the soul's preoccupation with itself. It is not a hope for the future, nor is it an interest in present details. Peace carries with it a surpassing of personality. There is an inversion of relative values. It is primarily a trust in the efficacy of Beauty. There is involved a grasp of infinitude, an appeal beyond boundaries. Its emotional ef-fect is the subsidence of turbulence which inhibits. It preserves the springs of energy, and at the same time masters them for the avoid-ance of paralyzing distractions. The experience of Peace is largely

34. Hajime Nakamura, "Unity and Diversity in Buddhism," pp. 381–382.
35. Keiji Nishitani, "The Awakening of Self in Buddhism," p. 3.
36. E. R. Sarathchandra, *Buddhist Psychology of Perception*, p. 99. Also the identity of peace and Nibbana is in Robert H. L. Slater, *Paradox and Nirvana*, p. 113.
37. Kenneth K. Inada, "The Metaphysics of Buddhist Experience and the Whiteheadian Encounter," p. 484.

beyond the control of purpose. It comes as a gift. It enlarges the field of attention. Thus Peace is self-control at its widest, at the width where the 'self' has been lost, and interest has been transferred to coordinations wider than personality. It is largely for this reason that Peace is so essential for civilization. It is the barrier against narrowness. It is a positive feeling which crowns the life and motion of the soul.[38]

In this transcendence of the personal, Hartshorne attests, there is "an escape from the agonies of egotism in a kind of 'Nirvana'; this peace is the essential reward of virtue."[39]

Nothing in the fullness and totality of whatever is really real is inherently incapable of becoming incarnate in the passing moment of the live creature's encounter with the varied wonder and splendor of this world. The fullness of reality is accessible in its wholeness to every transitory now; it is intuited in our peak experiences without fail, but the artificial world we have created for ourselves reduces the range of our awareness to the paltry wavelength of an ego-centered, culture-encapsulated world. Amid the stress of contemporary life, who has the time, apart from the pressures of making a living, keeping the job, satisfying spouse and family, and trying to make sense of the events which the media select out of billions upon billions of events occurring throughout the globe? Who has an interest beyond the material comforts and the need everyone concedes for a higher standard of living? Who is disposed to hear a person say, as Whitehead does, that "our experience, dim and fragmentary as it is, yet sounds the utmost depths of reality?"[40]

Influences that predominate in the present world induce everyone to draft the whole world in his or her service, forcing every living moment into that ego-centered mould, tear-

38. Alfred North Whitehead, *Adventures of Ideas*, pp. 367–368.
39. Charles Hartshorne, *Creative Synthesis and Philosophic Method*, p. 308.
40. Alfred North Whitehead, *Science and the Modern World*, p. 18.

ing each moment from the living undifferentiated aesthetic fullness of reality, drawing the whole world into the far-flung designs impressed by the video-culture upon all, draining thereby the reality and value from life. These people are the transmission belts, the cultural agencies, of what we call the contemporary world. Their intuitive powers have long since been extinguished. No voice warns them against sacrificing their lives; they are dropouts from the continuing struggle to give fuller birth to the lavish, aesthetically breathtaking world. They are "backworldsmen," with no foreground, no becoming.

The Buddhist perspective speaks the deepest truth about our lives, that the destiny for which we are fitted is the unlimited harmony of the widest variety of contrasts, the unity of authentic differences in the aesthetic matrix of life. The Nirvana-oriented life shifts the perspective of conventional wisdom by opening the individual to, as Guenther puts it, "the aesthetic experience that ultimately can lead to the enlightenment as an abiding peak experience."[41] This experience is never distributed wholesale, but to only one individual at a time. There is an ancient tale of the Buddha holding a man's head under water until he almost was drowned for lack of air; then releasing him, saying, "When you are as needful of knowledge as you just were for air, come back and be my disciple." Nirvana remains an impenetrable mystery until we feel ourselves suffocating from the parochial and provincial limits in which we have been reared. Nirvana is won only by one who breaks the grip of the familiar; it is hidden from those who believe that one lives best with people of our own age, social class, occupation, and ethnic tradition; it is hidden when people say to one another that they live least well among people with whom they differ. Nirvana is perceived only by men and women whose enthusiasm for sharing the values of their contemporaries has come to a wounded and lonely end. It is then

41. Herbert V. Guenther, *Buddhist Philosophy in Theory and Practice*, p. 178.

that the work begins, the loosening of attachments in order to locate one's identity, once and for all time, in the infinite fecundity, the strangeness, the beauty in the vivid flow of life itself.[42]

42. Here, as elsewhere in the present chapter, we see that, as G. C. Pande says, "Paṭicca-samuppāda and Nibbāna are the two sides or aspects of the Dhamma" (*Studies in the Origins of Buddhism*, p. 465). Stcherbatsky remarks of his book, *The Conception of Buddhist Nirvana*, "It can be regarded as a sister volume [to my *Central Conception of Buddhism*] and could have also borne 'the title of The Central Conception of Mahayana'" (preface of the Nirvana volume).

5

~~~~~~~~~~~~~~~~~~~~~~~~~~~~~~~~

Freedom in the Buddhist Perspective

He who wants to follow the Path of the Buddha must give up all thoughts of "I" and "mine." But this giving up does not make us poorer; it actually makes us richer, because what we renounce and destroy are the walls that kept us imprisoned; and what we gain is that supreme freedom, according to which every individual is essentially connected with all that exists, thus embracing all living beings in his own mind, taking part in their deepest experience, sharing sorrow and joy.

> *Lama Anagarika Govinda*
> *The Psychological Attitude*
> *of Early Buddhist Philosophy*

BY FAR THE MOST prodigal waste of life in this living world stems from that frightening form of provincialism described by Whitehead as being endemic to the West:

For three centuries European learning has employed itself in a limited task. Scholars, in science and in literature, have been brilliantly successful. But they have finished that task—the possession of clear ideas, woven into compound structures, with the attributes either of truth, or of beauty, or of moral elevation. European learning was founded on the dictionary; and splendid dictionaries were produced. With the culmination of the dictionaries the epoch has ended. For this reason, all the dictionaries of all the languages have failed to provide for the expression of the full human experience. Learning is sensible, straightforward, and clear, if only you keep at bay the suggestiveness of things. Experience does not occur in the clothing of verbal phrases. Even methods are limitations.[1]

The legacy of European learning impresses upon the minds of men and women everywhere the conclusions which a few tens of thousands—almost exclusively nonpigmented, male, middle-class, and Occidental—have found helpful in their drive for values. We of this universe are now confronted with the task of freeing life on this good earth from these assumptions and one-sided perspectives which have carried the baton of civilization during the last three hundred years, assumptions and viewpoints which have placed the fertility of human experience at large under a strange enthrallment to second- and third-hand conclusions regarding the nature and meaning of life.

Without even knowing the billions of people who are constantly ingesting their assumptions and one-sided conclusions, these unchosen socially-active leaders of the age of science and technology have become during our own time among the most dangerous men and women to whom the nurturing earth has given life. For in accepting the generalizations drawn by their half-knowledge, their one-sided values and culture-bound conclusions, the West has attempted to ban from the memory of humankind forever the intuitions and joyful forms of awareness which the multitudes of non-European people experience during fugitive moments in the unconventional-ized depths of their lives. The fact that the attempts are for the most part without deliberate intent diminishes not a whit the possible power of those leaders to erase from the future the experiences which the vast majority of humankind might contribute to the qualitative enrichment of the planet.

This is the present crisis of freedom in the contemporary world, and it is unlikely that the planet's population can cope with this problem unless the perspectives and methods elaborated in the Buddhist tradition for over two thousand years can be brought into sharper focus than a century of largely European scholarship has managed to achieve.

1. Alfred North Whitehead, *Science and Philosophy*, pp. 225, 226, 235.

The chief role of Buddhism now is to increase the freedom men and women can enjoy from the pathological compulsions of life. The Buddhist legacy is prepared to participate in opening the lives of millions to new flexibility in discovering the meaning of life, thus providing ways of curing people of the egocentricity and narcissism that mount to pathological heights of self-worship in some parts of the present world. It is equipped with methods that have stood the test for centuries to diminish the suffering that is possibly more intense than at any previous time. The Buddhist tradition can provide millions of people with an alternative orientation more suitable for exercising the self-corrective creativity with which they have all been endowed by the inexhaustible fecundity of nature.

If Buddhism is to fulfill this role, its perspective must be clarified regarding the nature of human suffering, its roots in false views of the self and personal identity, and the methods whereby people can be freed for the more abundant life. Just as the whole medieval outlook in the West had to be abandoned by men and women who became sponsors of the age of science and technology, so now Buddhism has the historic opportunity of assisting in the establishment of a new civilization, unrestricted by the systems of corporate belief and practice that distinguish the contemporary world.

Buddhism is ready to give positive reinforcement to millions of people who have already moved beyond the limited horizons of the superindustrial age. The constant intercourse between all nations and races, the perception of the good earth from outer space, and the new insights regarding the way creativity increases in the experience of humanity have all played a part in moving such post-modern people to the point where they are less tempted than their counterparts of a century ago to control their lives in the habit-ridden pathways of the cultures to which they belong. They are no longer capable of using existing cultural artifacts and abstractions in the ways that have given the twentieth century its infamous title as the century of the great world wars. They are psychologically, socially, and religiously prepared to attend to the Buddhist focus on suffering, particularly since their own sentiments no longer permit them to dismiss impoverishments suffered now as experiences compensated for "in the long run" or "in a higher realm" beyond the grave.

Buddhist views on freedom, suffering, and the nature of personal identity are relevant as never before in history to these more-than-modern pioneers of a new age, whose lives are constantly threatened with a reduction in the range of awareness. Social and cultural pioneering is in evidence everywhere in the contemporary world—in hundreds of small-group innovations designed to vivify and expand the spectrum of personal experience, in thousands of books and periodicals published in hopes of generating more power of self-assertion and less servility to ancestral ways, and in therapies too numerous to mention. Theodore Roszak's latest book groups all of these experiments toward new cultural horizons under the title, "The Aquarian Frontier." There is, Roszak writes, a greater-than-bourgeois need. It is "our need to become *serious* human beings, people who grow by virtue of having struggled in the solitude of the heart to find both moral dignity and personal meaning. It is our need to live deeply, to take life in our hands, to weigh and feel it, to give it deliberate shape—our *own* shape, the shape of our peculiar experience."[2]

One of these social and cultural experiments was presented during prime-time television by the National Broadcasting Company on July 21, 1978, in the form of a documentary film by Edwin Newman bearing the significant title, "I Want It All Now." Life in one of the ten wealthiest counties in the United States—Marin County, California—was shown with its proliferation of therapy groups, creature comforts, and various new ways of concentrating on "the perfection of the self." The rule of narcissism in a county with what Newman called "a tremendous obsession with Self" attracted people from thousands of miles away. In a population of 220,000, there are over 100 psychiatrists, 1 for every 2,000 people (including children, of which there are fewer than the national norm). All institutions in Marin County seem to be involved in the

2. Theodore Roszak, *Unfinished Animal*, p. 37.

search for new ways of "remaking and enhancing the happiness of the self." Homes are nestled in scenes of natural beauty and are valued in a range exceeding $100,000.

Statistics indicate, however, that experiments in Marin County may be reinforcing the culture-encapsulation and ego-centeredness the inhabitants seek to overcome. A few were leaving who found the social experiment a failure, as evidenced in the highest alcohol consumption in the nation, the highest divorce rate anywhere on record, and twice the national rate of suicide. One woman preparing to leave in her new station wagon was asked to explain the high suicide rate. Commenting upon the beauty of the surrounding countryside, its coastal range of mountains, and the wealth of the community, she said, "It is a kind of end-of-the-rainbow encounter which says to everyone, 'If you can't be happy here, life is probably no good anywhere.'"

The contemporary world brings into its social adventures the assumptions that underlie its one-sided, consumer-oriented values. Experiments now going on everywhere in the United States, similar to the one in Marin County, are not likely to discover the key that will unlock the problems of freedom, suffering, and personal identity, chiefly because this key can be found, as I said in the preceding chapter, only by men and women whose enthusiasm for sharing the values of their contemporaries has come to a wounded and lonely end. It was just such adventures in solitariness that opened a new way in the cultural wilderness more than twenty-six centuries ago, when the maharaja's eldest son, Siddhartha, abandoned the luxuriant grounds of a high caste Hindu palace at Kapilavastu in Northern India near the Nepal border, to explore an initial compassion for the suffering he witnessed on brief visits to the world beyond the palace grounds. Northrop sums up this "abandonment":

Instead of riding in his chariot with military pomp and splendor along the Royal Highway, deferred to by those of the higher castes, while those of lower caste, the aged, the hungry, the crippled, the diseased, the beggars and the untouchables, were pushed to the rear or out of sight beyond concern—instead, he put on the humble

person's simple garb—a single cotton sheet draped around his body—
to seek out, face objectively, and share with fellow-feeling the bodily ills and pains of his fellow men. He thereby cultivated, first in
himself and then in others, the natural compassion for all living
creatures that such understanding and shared pain and suffering
elicit.[3]

The bridge to the future is perceived and trod by people, people
like Nietzsche's Zarathustra, to whom a new way of remaining true to the earth has been communicated in their most
silent and solitary hour.[4]

FREEDOM FROM SUFFERING

Nothing characterizes Buddhism more than its sensitive
awareness and infinite compassion for human pain and suffering. The Buddha left the comfortable confinement of a young
wife, a new son, and an ancestral home to struggle and teach
for half a century, until he had placed deliverance from suffering within the reach of individual men and women everywhere on earth. The famous Four Noble Truths deal with this
universality of suffering and its cure. Suffering, the First Noble
Truth says, is an inescapable part of the human condition in
the most primitive and the most fully modernized nations of
the world. Suffering, the Second Truth says, has an intelligible cause; there is nothing mysterious about it; the cause is
the irresistible tendency of people everywhere to allow some
passion or drive, some anonymous schedule of habit or routine, some socially coercive role and class to rise to dominance
over all that can be thought and felt and done. Suffering has
its causal matrix in the inveterate clinging and craving,
grasping and possessing, hungering and hoping which become pathological under the ordinary conditions of human life.
Suffering comes from trying to live against the grain, to live
for the satisfaction of some over-ruling want or drive and thus

3. F. S. C. Northrop, "Naturalistic Realism and Animate Compassion,"
p. 174.
4. See Friedrich Nietzsche, *Thus Spake Zarathustra*, pp. 6–7.

to ignore the most powerful motivation of all, the need to be faithful to the fundamental creativity of life.

The Third Noble Truth asserts that suffering can be overcome by methods of analytic and meditative behavior which break the grip of all compulsive striving, widen the range and vivify the flow of quality in the passing moment, and awaken the individual to the rich and deep aesthetic center of life. The Fourth Truth is an elaboration of the Way, the Eightfold Path, in which suffering is overcome.

Driven behavior—constrained, unconscious, without alternative courses of action—is the central emphasis in the Buddha's analysis of suffering. Unconsciously motivated behavior afflicts all men and women until they have embarked successfully upon the path of purification.[5] The norm for human behavior, according to the Buddha, is complete transparency as regards the deeper-than-conscious motivations which exploit all powers of thought and perception. The underlying flow of vivid, undifferentiated quality at the center of life is blocked and turned into neurotic—that is, rigid and compulsive—demands. Even charitable deeds may be done out of this servitude to suffering, each culture-world having its own special forms of derailing resentment and placing suffering in the most favorable light. Lawrence S. Kubie, for example, believes there to be

no culture of which we have any knowledge which has solved the problem of how to bring up its children free from neurotic distortions. They make up the universal masked neurotic components of what we euphemistically call "normal" human psychology. Man's development has always been limited by the fact that his preconscious functions become trapped between, on the one hand, the pedestrian, halting, earth-bound, reality-oriented processes of conscious symbolic representation, and, on the other, the neurotic distortions of symbolic processes which are imposed by unconscious conflicts and the secondary and tertiary consequences. Education itself is caught between the two. If we are to do anything about this problem we must view it ontogenetically, starting perhaps by ac-

5. See Nolan Pliny Jacobson, "Purification and Pollution in Buddhism."

knowledging our past culpable indifference to the child's early loss of free and spontaneous creative zest. When he learns to use words, even before formal education starts, he becomes less free, because words themselves confine the pre-conscious stream. Our educational processes tend to destroy the creative potential of a large share of those who survive.[6]

The Buddha's therapeutic, pragmatic approach to suffering has been elaborated two millenia later in the West in both Freudian and non-Freudian orientations, in both existential and nonexistential psychiatries. Carl Rogers finds within all individuals, for example, an unwillingness to have the character and direction of their lives decided by conditions they cannot perceive and understand. When individuals examine their situation and feel that they have discovered what is wrong, they insist upon undertaking the control and direction of their own lives on the ultimately rewarding path of qualitative growth.[7]

In its concern with suffering, Buddhism belongs in the contemporary world, as a powerful intercepter of its most self-destructive trends. Buddhism has something to say to people whose lives get caught in habit-ridden, compulsive, conformist, ego-centered and culture-encapsulated forms of behavior before they realize what has taken place. In its diagnosis of suffering and its cure, Buddhism belongs *especially* in the contemporary world, for here people live in varying degrees of awareness that if they are going to participate in the prevailing forms of life they face the certain prospect of becoming increasingly programmed, scheduled, fragmented, and mobilized under the demands of a burgeoning technology moving with a momentum of its own. Exposed night and day to the growing unpredictability of life amid explosive change, they mistake the direction from which the mortal danger comes. Not knowing that the resources required for curing their pathological disorders must be found within themselves, they

6. Lawrence S. Kubie, "Unsolved Problems of Scientific Education," pp. 97–98.
7. Carl Rogers, *Client-Centered Therapy*, p. 490.

seek their emancipation in the very lifestyles that threaten the continuance of the superindustrial age. Every step taken into the higher positions of leadership removes them another unbridgeable distance from the aesthetic center in their own experience. The prisons are already in place before they awaken to the diminishing quality and growing meaninglessness of their lives—confinements associated with their drive for power and prestige, or with the well-defined community regard for people of great wealth, or with some other laudable ambition, such as becoming a reputable scientist or scholar. "It was reserved for Buddhist insight," Paul Masson-Oursel has written, "to discern the servitude in good as in evil: to find egotism in traditional religion, in enjoyment, and in gain."[8]

Impermanent beings in a changing world, people hang like leeches to some part of the world, even if they have to invent something to cling to. Their minds look for harbors in which to stabilize the kaleidoscope of perceptions and events. A system of habits appears to give stability and permanence to a transitory world, and people disregard all the small clues that their lives are becoming more abstract, that they are losing penetrative power, and that their capacity for spontaneity and fellow feeling is diminishing with each passing year. There are many things about the contemporary world that remain a puzzle, but no one need wonder that human personality, robbed of its living roots, and shaped in these pathological ways, should become capable of cruelty beyond description, beyond dramatization, even beyond science fiction. Nuclear proliferation— including the capacity of some countries for vast overkill— and revolutions which exchange one tyranny for another are two of the few remaining predictable features of life in the superindustrial age.

All of this constitutes an appalling tale of suffering, of lives whose native power of expansiveness has been lost, and of constantly growing inability to make contact with the deep productivity of experience itself. *Tanhā* ("compulsive power") keeps lives such as these from establishing organic ties with

8. Paul Masson-Oursel, "Indian Techniques of Salvation," p. 208.

the flow of quality out of the foundations of the world. "Over-powering forces" and "general defilements" control every-one's behavior, until the light dawns that emancipation de-pends entirely upon oneself. Humans are tragic figures who rarely are able to go along with the rhythms within their own bodies and within the natural matrix which they inhabit for a time with others.

Every culture up to now has misled human development in this fundamental way, teaching men and women to exploit the living moments that are already theirs, using them to serve some goal or good, some glorified image of what life might become, some vision of the larger scheme of things, some phase of the world considered more basic than all else, or some clus-ter of their own total drives, always in the expectation that the result will prove to be an improvement over the creativity operating in the sensitive core of their existence. The few breakthroughs that elicit widespread and powerful response from time to time sooner or later fall under the control of the self-serving institutions of the age. No poetry, nor painting, nor literature with the cutting edge of tragedy in its heart seems capable of sustaining for long an awareness of what is taking place—either in the rising generations or their elders, or in any ethnic, racial, or national tradition. The modern Pro-metheus batters unavailingly against the superior power and enthrallment of his cultural trap.

FREEDOM FROM THE SELF

The most powerful prison of forced striving is the self, that most fundamental of all illusions identified by the Buddha. Nonidentical, independent, substantial selves confront for-ever the task of preserving their own identity in the face of volatile change, and they have the equally impossible task of discovering some creative ground for unity with other sub-stantial selves. When Nāgārjuna saw that "the tendency to seize is the root of conflict and suffering,"[9] the source of this

9. See K. Venkata Ramanan, *Nāgārjuna's Philosophy*, p. 38.

tendency was located in the notion of an independently existing self.

In his doctrine of *anattā* ("egolessness"), the Buddha confronts the organizing principle of all compulsive, proprietary striving. He teaches that as we penetrate towards concrete apprehension, the seemingly permanent limits between persons and things disappear, leaving no self as the object of concern and the center of reality-oriented drives.

Setting out to solve the problem of Suffering [Pande affirms], Buddha discovered its answer in that transcendental illusion under the force of which our minds construct for themselves a stable universe of separate individuals and substances, finite "selves" and objects, where life is spent in the unavailing pursuit of phantasms. Depending on a beginning-less Ignorance, arise Name-and-Form, a world of individual persons and things, and depending on this arises experience by way of contact, and thence pleasure and pain, love and hate. Craving and striving, "we" lay down the weary burden of one life only to pick up that of another. Thus moves on the impersonal process of Suffering, uncreated, but contingent. It ceases when Nirvāṇa is attained.[10]

Unconscious motivational drives attach themselves to the self for three reasons: first, because the indeterminacy at the center of a person's being, the possibilities for unlimited and ultimate growth, can be felt as troublesome; second, because this substantial self is an infection spread from one generation to the next, without ever reaching conscious awareness; and, third, because a pseudoself once concealing the truth must be defended at all costs, lest anxiety over the indeterminacy of life may rise to dominance despite all that has been done to suppress it.

The nature of one's own identity and experience having become falsified by the illusion of a permanent self, the dualisms of life proliferate. The self is here; the environment is there; and the bifurcating self transmits forever the confrontations of man and nature, mind and body, nature and life, matter and spirit, nature and culture, time and eternity, form and

10. G. C. Pande, *Studies in the Origins of Buddhism*, p. 511.

formless forever. The fragmentation and anarchy of life in the contemporary world thus have deep and apparently incurable assumptions regarding the nature of experience at the human level.

William James confronted in Buddhist fashion the same illusory nature of the self. Gordon Allport confirms: "There is, [James] thinks, no such thing as a substantive self distinguishable from the sum total, or stream, of experiences. Each moment of consciousness, he says, appropriates each previous moment, and the knower is thus somehow embedded in what is known."[11] James found reasons for believing that the self is not the "skin-enclosed" entity we think but a process unlimited to its immediate matrix of life. Each moment of consciousness, James argued, is part of a stream, each moment appropriating previous "cells of experience" in a process that never ends.

All one has to do is to notice what is felt. Feelings undulate forever in our neural networks, and we "know" what the world is like from the way it "feels." We devise methods and logics for checking on the feelings, but these are likewise somewhat different feelings too. All ideas, James argued, are rooted in feeling. Our memories, moreover, are also rooted in feeling; we literally feel our memories. We *are*, therefore, this series of feelings—some inherited from the past, some presently going on, some orienting us toward the future. Our most inclusive self is the most recent self, numerically new at any given moment. It may not effectively embrace and include every one of its predecessors, but it can tell which events belong in its own series and which belong in the series of another person. This most inclusive self, inclusive of the fullest range of variety in its feelings of past and present and future, *experiences* the process of being alive in this way. James puts it succinctly:

Individuality is founded in feeling; and the recesses of feeling, the darker, blinder strata of character, are the only places in the world in which we catch real fact in the making, and directly perceive how events happen, and how work is actually done. Compared

11. Gordon Allport, *Becoming*, p. 51.

with this world of living individualized feelings, the world of generalized objects which the intellect contemplates is without solidity
or life. As in stereoscopic or kinetoscopic pictures seen outside the
instrument, the third dimension, the movement, the vital element,
are not there.[12]

Whitehead illustrates in the following way the viewpoint
James had pioneered. Objecting to the way Descartes'
famous *cogito ergo sum* has been translated and transmitted to
every student of philosophy in the West, Whitehead argues
that

it is never bare thought or bare existence that we are aware of.
I find myself as essentially a unity of emotions, enjoyments, hopes,
fears, regrets, valuations of alternatives, decisions—all of them
subjective reactions to the environment as active in my nature. My
unity—which is Descartes' "I am"—is my process of shaping this
welter of material into a consistent pattern of feelings. The individual enjoyment is what I am in my role of a natural activity, as I
shape the activities of the environment into a new creation, which
is myself at this moment; and yet, as being myself, it is a continua-
tion of the antecedent world. If we stress the role of the environment, this process is causation. If we stress the role of my immediate pattern of active enjoyment, this process is self-creation. If
we stress the role of the conceptual anticipation of the future whose
existence is a necessity in the nature of the present, this process is
the teleological aim at some ideal in the future. This aim, however,
is not really beyond the present process. For the aim at the future
is an enjoyment in the present. It thus effectively conditions the
immediate self-creation of the new creature.[13]

The indeterminate future becomes the determinate past. The
way the past perishes is the way the future becomes. All that
is real is the moment as it passes. The foundations of the world
are encountered in every individual capable of noting the way
experience, as James put it, "comes in drops."

The base line of personal identity is not the substantial self
with its *svabhāva* ("own nature"), existing from the first mo-

12. William James, *The Varieties of Religious Experience*, pp. 501–502. See
also his *Essays in Radical Empiricism*, especially chapters 2, 5, and 6.
13. Alfred North Whitehead, *Modes of Thought*, p. 166.

ment of its career and ready to acquire and contain changing properties as it lives. Personal identity is found in the process of aesthetic enrichment enabling us to inherit more perceptively and vividly the legacy of qualities experienced in the past. The identity and order of an individual's life is either found in these passing moments—since they are all that is really real—or thrown overboard, one imperceptible dribble at a time.

Each passing moment, every actuality, is an occasion of experience with its own unity, the outcome of its own synthesizing of the many events of the past into the novel emergent now. There is no other unity from which the oneness of the momentary experience can be derived. It has nothing as its object; it is self-enjoyed; it is self-created; and, in turn, it becomes a part of the permanent past, ready for another momentary experience to gather it up into another novel synthesis tomorrow. The fleeting moment possesses nothing, is contained by nothing, simply and fundamentally *is*. It is free, therefore, to feel and to celebrate life as it synthesizes fleeting moments out of its own series of preceding events or out of some other person's individual strand of becoming.

No "nonidentity," therefore, ever separates fellow creatures from one another when the bifurcating self, through analysis and meditation, disappears as a determinant of life. This is the basis for both personal identity and compassion in the Buddhist orientation. *Khaṇa-vāda* ("fleeting events") either fall into more or less definite strands of becoming, which Whitehead calls "societies," with the self creating its identity as it goes, or the self of each person is inescapably nonidentical with those of its fellow creatures, including those of all creatures in the ecosystem of life. In the first alternative— the Buddhist perspective—people form their identities as social facts in the course of their own growth through the *khaṇa-vāda* of their lives. In the latter alternative—the self-centered, culture-encapsulated way of the contemporary world—individuals find their own experiences forever threatened with fragmentation and their natural nonidentity with other lives a continuing preparation for authoritarian rule.

With more conscious recognition than Whitehead had that he was confirming a very ancient Buddhist orientation, Peirce was first to give the Buddhist perspective on personal identity a clear formulation in the West. "All communication from mind to mind," he writes, "is through continuity of being. The selfhood you like to attribute to yourself is, for the most part, the vulgarest delusion of vanity. The barbaric conception of personal identity must be broadened. A man's spirit is embodied in others and continues to live and breathe and have its being very much longer than superficial observers think." He puts it more strongly still: "Your neighbors are, in a measure, yourself, and in far greater measure than you would believe."[14] *This* is the Bodhisattva Ideal.

Hartshorne has spent a lifetime in the endeavor to show that personal identity is stronger in this perspective which frees individuals to synthesize relevant momentary experiences without regard for whether they occurred in one historic series or another. "It is the philosophical glory of Buddhism," Hartshorne writes, "that it saw through the relativity of substantial identity long, long ago. Altruism is as directly grounded in the nature of the self as is self-interest. My awareness of my past tends to be more vivid and direct than the awareness of the past of others, but this is no absolute difference." Elsewhere he states:

In the Buddhist-Whiteheadian view nothing is real but individuals—on the human level, conscious individuals. Groups are not such individuals. But neither are egos, as single entities there for sixty years. No such ego is ever literally "conscious of itself." The self-now is the individual subject actually enjoying the present consciousness; later selves will enjoy it so far as they anticipated it. Any "timelessly the same" self, birth to death, is a mere abstraction. It does not literally do or know anything. The Buddhist "no-soul" doctrine makes it possible literally to love the other as oneself, i.e., as not another substance.[15]

14. *Collected Papers of Charles Sanders Peirce*, vol. 7, pars. 571, 573.
15. Charles Hartshorne, "Personal Identity from A to Z," p. 213; idem, *The Logic of Perfection*, p. 122.

Because of just such a self, compassion in the Buddhist perspective has the cumulative process of personal growth on its side, because it takes into account the concreteness of what is really real in each individual's unconditional regard for definiteness, difference, particularity, and thus enables an individual *through compassion and love* to discover what is concretely the case, what is actually going on in the world. In the self-encapsulated way of the contemporary world, on the other hand, we fly in the face of what is most real when we ask individuals to treat other people as themselves.

Unifying itself in each passing moment by embracing all its predecessors through memory and perception, each self has natural, compassionate relations with selves not in its own series, and people in the Buddhist view are forever "members one of another." This is why Govinda could say that "the extremes of identity or non-identity" are excluded forever in Buddhist thought, and why the concept of relational origination (or conditioned genesis) discussed in chapter 2 shows itself to be "the necessary counterpart of the anattā-idea, the doctrine of no soul or substantial self which emphasizes the character of life and growth, in contrast to the fossilized concept of an absolute entity which would logically call for similarly absolute (lifeless) laws."[16] People either form their identities as social facts in the course of their growth from one fleeting instant to the next, or all appeals to their possible "self-interest" in taking others as objects of mutual concern must ultimately fail. As Hartshorne indicates, each member in a series is self-enjoyed rather than self-interested, even the self of the future being "also another."[17]

The perspective that the momentary experiences with their qualitative richness are cumulative, indeed *never* evacuated or lost from further experience, enables Buddhists to move with more confidence in creation than is normal in the contempo-

16. Lama Anagarika Govinda, *The Psychological Attitude of Early Buddhist Philosophy*, pp. 56–57.
17. Harshorne, *The Logic of Perfection*, p. 122. See also his *Creative Synthesis and Philosophic Method*, p. 198; also p. 76: "The given world is the enjoyed and suffered world."

rary world, with no fear of being encapsulated in any ego- or culture-centered conclusions about life. At the end of a period of strenuous personal reorientation, experimentation, and discovery of appropriate methods of meditation, any person of moderate intelligence, health, and vitality will acknowledge that a life of rich consummatory experience in the fulfilled now is not to be traded for a life compulsively committed to established beliefs and belongings. People are predisposed by their strenuous reorientation to give up the idea that substances are the most concrete items of reality, and are prepared to find life where it really is—in the concrete qualitative flow whose vivification and intensification is capable of making each "momentary state" or "truly singular event" memorable forever. These singular events become, rather than change, and constitute the only apparent cure for the dominant viewpoints of the contemporary world, because they enable us to participate in feelings as they are being synthesized in our own experience *before* the categories of the understanding can apply distinctions and draw inferences in ways that leave the organic wholeness of life in fragments which must seek, consciously or otherwise, for violent and despotic means of coordination.

There may well be an infinity of possibly better worlds, but to the Buddhist each one can bring only a harvest of suffering when the experience from which it takes its departure has been treated, either in oneself or others, with disdain, disapproval, or inquisitorial threat. The more we attend to what is actually taking place in the fleeting moments of our own experience, moments that are gone before anyone can take them fully into account, the more we become aware that they constitute the canvas on which the portrait of our lives is embedded. Each moment, for good or evil, we are putting the finishing touches on this portraiture of our lives, and it is the purest embodiment of unreason to ignore or disclaim the concrete artistic creation each individual can contribute to the world's life. This is the very soul of suffering: that each fleeting moment as it perishes is mangled as another is born. And it is the essence of ignorance to dream of new horizons and new worlds before we have awakened to the events-in-process out of which all worlds emerge. To cure the suffering we need a change in attitudes, points of view, ways of experiencing the world; and the Buddhist legacy offers for this purpose the method of freedom—meditation.

This is the heart of the Buddha's Enlightenment, where he came to see that what has no independent existence loses its grip over humankind. Everything in the world creates itself as it passes and becomes a part of a new creation. Nothing holds the experiences together except the experiences themselves in their various forms of togetherness. The substantial self, no longer required to "have" and to "hold" experiences together, loses all relevance for inquiry, and does not become the compulsive "tendency to seize" which Nāgārjuna considered the root of conflict and bondage. In its place, we discover in moments of growing awareness the nature of our own nuclear experience with its cohesive power to link each of us to all others, and humankind to all other forms of life. This is the Buddhist assertion hurled across the gulfs of the contemporary world. The world awaits a race of men who will treasure the living moment without insisting that it live forever, in *bare attention* experiencing its vivid flow. This living moment is where each person forever is, and it is incomparably more than can ever be thought or spoken. Since the living moment of qualitative richness at the center of life is neither a cognitive act, nor a reflection over something considered superior to sensate bodily existence, the silence of the Buddha has always been remembered as his own response to the bottomlessness of his Enlightenment.

FREEDOM TO CREATE

It is one of the surpassing wonders of the orientations and perspectives of humankind that a world whose many-splendored patterns rise and fall, come into experience and retire into the past with neither beginning nor end, should provide the fundamental conditions for freedom, while the forms of Western civilization are said to have been created "in the beginning," *ex nihilo*, and placed under humanity's stewardship and dominion, thereby stripping humanity and every other concrete unit of reality of all self-creative power, the forms having been laid down by the One from whom, after *the* act of Creation, all freedom and love and forms of togetherness and creativity must thereafter be procured. It is worth wondering, indeed, if in this initial condition of servility to omnipotent power Western civilization, where freedom has been almost continually on people's minds, may have committed itself forever to a world in which, not freedom, but tyranny must prevail.

In contrast to the accounts of creation in the West, Buddhism confers freedom upon all forms of life, from particles to protoplasm to the most distant star. All change is understood as the free and novel emergence of qualities that are forever new. It is, Hartshorne would argue, in these qualities of the fleeting instant, each incorporating the past in memory and perception, that people acquire their first lessons in what it means to be free, what it means to *become* in the ultimate form of growth.[18] This is what Malalasekera intended in his phrase "the fulfilled *Now*." It is here, in these fleeting instants, that Buddhism stands in solidarity with individuals fighting to safeguard whatever freedom and insight they have managed to salvage amid the senseless brutalities of the contemporary world. Buddhism is powerfully supportive of such people, who may be moving in cultural trends that leave more to the individual's discretion and control, and less to external constraints.

In the light of what has been said of the bifurcating self and the compulsive drivenness of the suffering creature, no one would think it a conundrum that freedom is called in question in many circles of modern science. Nature has shown itself to be divisible, and the suffering resulting from the fragmentation and alienation has been the necessary counterpart of the divisive drive for power. The cost in terms of grossly misunderstanding the interconnectedness of phenomena, however, and particularly the preventive and curative relations be-

18. Hartshorne, "Personal Identity from A to Z," p. 211.

tween humanity and its cultural matrix have now mounted to prohibitive levels. The fragmenting methods may have been essential, considering the limitations with which the modern mind began its investigations of nature from 1600 until the present. But the dangers have not been kept in mind, with the result that human freedom as experienced in the Buddhist perspective has been cut off more or less completely from the life of science in the contemporary world. (This is the theme of the chapter to follow.) What is lost, then, is the universal principle of reality and causation—the freedom to create.[19]

"It takes time," Hartshorne writes, "to outgrow so deeply fixed a habit as determinism represents for many. But the working physicists seem already largely to have outgrown it."[20] Hartshorne also writes of Whitehead:

For two thousand years the theologians and philosophers had attempted to deal with creative freedom as but a special or exceptional case of something else, such as causality. Whitehead makes the daring leap, less clearly outlined already by Lequier, Fechner, Bergson, Peirce, Berdyaev, and a few others, of making creativity itself the universal principle of reality and causation. Not just God creates, not even just God and man, but every concrete unit of re-

19. Charles Hartshorne, *Whitehead's Philosophy*, p. 132. Causation plays a central role in the Buddhist tradition. What I have called "the central conception" is itself a theory of causation (see chapter 3). "He who sees the nature of causation sees the dhamma, and he who sees the dhamma sees the nature of causation" (*The Middle Length Sayings, Majjhima-Nikāya*, vol. 1, p. 191). See also K. N. Jayatilleke, *Early Buddhist Theory of Knowledge*, pp. 454–455: "We cannot subscribe to Thomas' belief that in Buddhism causation was never applied as a 'universal philosophical principle,' . . . nor with R. E. Hume's remark that 'neither Buddha nor the Buddhist writings had any interest in problems of scientific causation.'" Jayatilleke here takes exception as well to C. A. F. Rhys Davids' remark that Buddhist causality "comes near to the Principle or Law of Sufficient Reason" since in some instances, notably in Leibniz, Jayatilleke continues, "the reasons cannot usually be known by men and this is an attempt to explain things in terms of final causes."

20. Hartshorne, *The Logic of Perfection*, p. 181. See also his *Creative Synthesis*, p. 294: "The real issue is *within* the causal idea, not between it and its negation. Maxwell, Peirce, Poincaré, and Boutroux understood this long ago, most physicists have some understanding of it now. But cultural lag is always to be reckoned with in philosophy."

ality has its own special kind and degree of creativity. To be is to create. To be is to be free.[21]

The habit of determinism, to which Hartshorne refers, is one, it should be emphasized, that Buddhism through its long tradition has never acquired. Each individual is creator of himself, his freedom limited only by the freedom of all the others. Every person has expectations which have been modified by past experience, and this is the concept of *karma*, but in the same orientation every passing moment has the privilege of deciding what shall be attempted in the nexus of millions of influences which come to focus in every opportunity for choice. Buddhist theory and practice constitute together a compassionate therapy designed to free men and women for fuller use of their constructive capabilities and talents.

Individuals are all responsible for the degree to which they are awake and aware and capable of responding to the wonder of being alive. Each passing moment is experienced as rich or poor, vivid with quality or captured by boredom and despair, depending upon the individual's readiness to participate in the qualitative richness of the here and now. If one's life is habit-ridden, if the circumstances that give rise to an act predetermine its seemingly endless repetition, the responsibility rests upon the individual alone. Freedom to respond goes with the responsibility for the response that is chosen.

The problem for Buddhism, therefore, is not whether man has been left a shred of freedom to create in a causally determined world. This issue was settled when the bifurcating consciousness of the substantial self was dismissed as illusion. The doctrine of *anattā* and the central conception of *pratītya-samutpāda* (*paṭicca-samuppāda*) settled this issue so decisively that in all the centuries of different schools of philosophy the issue has never been introduced. Buddhism took as its starting point the experience individuals undergo, and, as in the supportive philosophies of process now coming to dominance in the United States, the power of discrimination is exercised upon the experience itself, from which entities such as an ego

21. Hartshorne, *Whitehead's Philosophy*, pp. 132, 133.

are inferred. In the Buddhist-Whiteheadian starting point of inquiry, experience begins with a sense of power, the essence of this power being, to quote Whitehead, "the drive toward aesthetic worth for its own sake."[22] In important ways a clarification and elaboration of Whitehead and Peirce, Hartshorne's voluminous writings revolve around the thesis that creativity is inherent in experiencing as such, since "it is an aesthetic law of experiencing that without the unforeseen there can be no experience. To experience must be a free act, or nothing intelligible. We shall never understand life and the world until we see that the zero of freedom can only be the zero of experiencing, and even of reality."[23] Freedom to create is rooted in *reality as such*.

Buddhism's continuing encounter with the contemporary world comes at a time when science has less tendency to support the nineteenth-century notion that a person is causally determined in his behavior by genetic and socio-historical formations. The inherent tendency of the superindustrial age towards concentration of decision-making and authoritarian control appears to have lost the support of the very physical sciences which initially provided the deterministic picture of the Newtonian machine. The interests of a burgeoning industrial revolution were well served at the outset by the image of the world as a system ruled by universal causation. The categorization of mind and matter as separate entities held out for a time the promise that mathematical measurement would deliver colossal power of control. The present age with its global technological embrace may well have been impossible without the measuring and categorizing mentality that now finds itself exhausted in the quantum revolution that, to use George Gamow's phrase, "shook the world."[24] In connection with the discussion of "the central conception of Buddhism" in chapter 3, I quoted Stapp as now finding in the realm of elementary-particle physics the kind of spontaneity

22. Whitehead, *Modes of Thought*, p. 119.
23. Hartshorne, *Creative Synthesis*, pp. 306, 6.
24. See George Gamow, *Thirty Years That Shook Physics*.

and "reaching out to other things" that we find "in the realm of mind." Stapp goes on to confirm what I have emphasized— that "an experience cannot be analyzed into ultimate unanalyzable entities; to isolate an experience from its references is to destroy its essence; experiences must be viewed as parts of webs, whose parts are not defined except through their connections to the whole."[25]

The interrelatedness of all phenomena and the creative nature of the world are part of high-energy physics, as they have been the central conception of Buddhism for more than two thousand years. We are participants in a world continually in process of becoming, at any stage of which no limits can be placed upon, as Hartshorne phrases it, "the pervasiveness either of spontaneity or of feeling in nature." The world, Stapp declares, is either "fundamentally lawless or fundamentally inseparable,"[26] which means that self-active entities at all levels—whether at the level of the two hundred particles now thought to constitute the atom, or at the level of the cells of one's body, including the five billion in the brain— are participants in their next stages and radically influenced by the self-activity of all the others. Whitehead, speaking of just such levels, confirms the point:

There is the animal life with its central direction of a society of cells, there is the vegetable life with its organized republic of cells, there is the cell life with its organized society of molecules, there is the large-scale inorganic society of molecules with its passive acceptance of necessities derived from spatial relations, there is the infra-molecular activity which has lost all trace of the passivity of inorganic nature on a larger scale.[27]

The key notion of the new cosmology of which freedom, or creativity, or creative synthesis is the central fact was suggested by Whitehead: "The energetic activity considered in

25. Henry Peirce Stapp, "S-Matrix Interpretation of Quantum Theory," p. 1319.
26. Hartshorne, *Creative Synthesis*, p. 8; Stapp, "Quantum Theory," p. 1308.
27. Whitehead, *Modes of Thought*, p. 157.

physics is the emotional intensity entertained in life"—life in a world where no event can be solely and wholly the cause of another, and where each happening is a creative synthesis of perhaps millions of events, each acquiring its own determinate character in the past; life in a world where the many become everlastingly one and are increased by one.[28]

The Buddhist conception of relational origination has contained for over twenty centuries the two basic elements of the world view now emerging in high energy physics and quantum theory: namely, the unity and interrelatedness of all phenomena, and the dynamic character of everything that is the case (as Wittgenstein once defined "the world"). This view makes headway only slowly, however, in highly specialized areas where purposes are advanced by denying that life everywhere is self-enjoyed and capable of acquiring its own creative meaning and value.

The Buddhist legacy constitutes the world's longest and richest unambiguous affirmation of freedom. This is one more respect in which its encounter with the contemporary world is new, for if any error regarding Buddhist thought has been more widespread than all the others, it is the notion held by some nineteenth-century scholars that Buddhism teaches self-denial, self-abnegation, even complete evacuation of the self. The Buddhist position on the self is far more simple. It is that our self-centered, self-deluding, self-justifying ways are ontologically absurd and represent a futile effort to center life in an illusion. Freedom is a generic feature of life in a Buddhist orientation. Freedom is the spontaneous emergence of novelty in the unceasing transitoriness of life. Events are free when they are novel, nonrepetitive, and rich with aesthetic quality. The Buddhist tradition has advocated freedom in a sense more radical and verifiable than any other philosophical tradition, until Charles Peirce and William James opened a new vestibule into twentieth-century life. Experience, Peirce held, is not what analysis discovers but the raw material on which analysis works: "Experience is our only teacher; it takes

28. Ibid., p. 168; idem, *Process and Reality*, p. 21.

place by a series of surprises."[29] In the beginning was—not the Word, nor the Deed—the celebration of life. K. Venkata Ramanan sums up:

> To live in the world and yet be free from defilements,
> To retain individuality and yet be free from the false self,
> To work for the world and yet be free from pride and passion—
> This is the skillfulness of the Buddha.[30]

THE METHOD OF FREEDOM

Buddhists have always had far more reason than Marx for rejecting philosophies that merely interpret the world in different ways. The point for Buddhism has always been to change the world through meditation.

Through meditation one is freed from the compulsive grip of the goals and goods that take charge in the absence of what is really real, from habit-ridden days and anonymous schedules that rule over people who would not otherwise know what to do, from the stress of sustaining a commitment to cognitive structures that every community in the modern world expects its leaders to defend, and from the stress of acquisitive feelings, the confinements of the cultural bind, the pathology of lost vitality and power, and the general scatteredness, shallowness, fragmentation and paralyzing distractions that rob life of its integrity, balance, and sense of direction. Through meditation individuals discover their own personal freedom in the front line listening posts of the world's creative advance.

Meditation techniques foster freedom in sensitizing individuals to the widening and deepening range of quality foreshadowing the emergence of novel forms of togetherness, by enabling us to experience the joy of burgeoning quality swelling unceasingly in moments that are absolutely new, by conferring on us a zest for life born in these nonconceptual, nontheoretical apprehensions of reality, and by teaching us that, as essential as theory is to our deepening grasp of reality, we

29. *Collected Papers of Charles Sanders Peirce*, vol. 5, pars. 50, 51.
30. Ramanan, *Nāgārjuna's Philosophy*, p. 69.

have the deeper need to be free from all that is theoretical as well. Life is inexhaustibly complex. It must be responded to with more than understanding. "We need to be artists in living," as Hartshorne has recently written, "and Buddhist meditation has this as its purpose." Feeling the rhythm of new increments in the flow of quality at the vital center of our lives, we are in touch with the foundations of the world.

The Buddha is the man who awakened to the forced strivings of the encapsulated, bifurcating self and to those self-centered basic ills (*rāga, doṣa,* and *moha*—"greed," "hatred," and "delusion") and overpowering forces (*diṭṭhi, kāma, avijjā,* and *bhava*—"dogmatism," "sensuality," "ignorance," and "forced being") into which life is normally locked and bolted. The tradition originating beneath the pipal tree at Bodhagayā is a major resource in these unconscious compulsions that have reached their most irresistible power in the contemporary world.

Meditation is a rigorous discipline designed to deepen an individual's ontological togetherness with the inner workings of life, an achievement no culture-world can confer upon its members and no person can learn by reading a book. The Buddha used several words to define what is intended by the term "meditation"—*bhāvanā, citta visuddhi, samatha, samādhi,* and *ekaggatā* ("cultivation of mind," "purification," "calming the mind," "unifying various mental powers with the creativity that drives the world," and "concentration"). The Buddha knew that people experience a collapse of intelligence when motivations of greed, envy, lust, and an unreasoning defense of one's ignorance dominate their lives. Under conditions such as these, people lose the power to see things as they really are. "Practice meditation," the Buddha advised his only son, "and the contacts that have arisen will not continue to obsess your mind."

Elsewhere, the Buddha asks:

"What is the purpose of a mirror?"
"Its purpose is reflection, revered sir."
"Even so, Rāhula, a deed is to be done with the body only after repeated reflection; a deed is to be done with speech . . . with the

mind only after repeated reflection. . . . All those recluses and brahmans, Rāhula, who in the long past purified a deed of body, purified a deed of speech, purified a deed of mind, did so only after repeated reflection. . . . This is how you must train yourself, Rāhula.[31]

In meditation each compelling drive loses the coerciveness of its usual state by being absorbed into the total experience of life's immediate centered flow; it is thus freed for full and free integration into the total capacity of the organism for experiencing its own ultimate growth. Meditation, T. Magness points out, enables one to assimilate with complete poise the fact that "from the ultimate standpoint, man—or any living form whatsoever—is merely an interaction of certain forces which interlock and adhere into a certain shape and size for an extremely brief duration, breaking up and dissolving into intangibility incessantly, with no basis of permanent identity, shape, or size whatsoever."[32]

The Buddha was calling for a profound revolution in the ordering of life. He knew that the entire superstructure of society is unsound and in momentary conflict with reality, not because it is based upon the requirements of a particular social class or caste, but because it rests upon wants, hungers, and drives of a thousand kinds, all of which have one thing in common—they rule over us unrelentingly without our knowing. "Repeated reflection," as the Buddha taught his son, can bring this to an end. Buddhism would not have remained a viable orientation to life, and it would not now be in a fresh encounter with the contemporary world if its message had been addressed especially to people in certain circumstances and stages of cultural development. It is enjoying a renaissance today because it deals creatively with humankind's central problem—on the one hand, its unlimited capacity for widening and deepening the range of its awareness, but, on the other, its inveterate tendency to live encompassed by forms that threaten us with an evolutionary dead end. The Buddha

31. *Middle Length Sayings (Majjhima-Nikāya)*, vol. 1, pp. 416, 420.
32. T. Magness, *Sammā Samādhi*, pp. 46–47.

speaks of a victory he has discovered over the proprietary consciousness of humankind, and so he speaks of "the mind without attachment," the mind undriven, uncompelled, unconstrained by unconscious motivation, the mind not fallen into apathy or dejection through restlessness and distraction, the mind "faring along not grasping anything in the world."[33] By freeing the mind in these ways we unite with all that is real in the world as we experience in conditioned genesis—as discussed in chapter 3—the relational power that belongs to no restricted strand or strain in the organic wholeness of life. We relate to the universe in its fullness with an openness only the most rigorous techniques of meditation can achieve. Power exercised apart from this fullness of existence predisposes people to violence and authoritarian rule.

Meditation is not essentially a mysterious business; it is not, however, an easy business. It is like clearing new ground, pulling up trees along with root systems that sometimes go very deep, and eradicating briar patches of sharp thorns that pierce sensitive skin. The uprooting of the wild patches is but the first step, as any farmer knows. New crops are to be grown where once deep undergrowth choked the most cautious intention. What begins to happen, however, in the disciplined course of meditation is that fresh bits of awareness emerge, insights that are ready to serve as wider angles of perception on what seems to be going wrong in our world. Up out of the smothered and forgotten underground of our experience the new intuitions come, and they come in more reliable form and in greater numbers the more diligently the meditation is pursued. Intuitions are part of the undercurrent of life, lying deeper than any form of understanding can probe. And from the Buddhist position they make the difference to which anything new in our situation can be traced.

Meditation thus opens us to a dimension of our experience beyond even our assumptions and presuppositions or convictional commitments. Long experience in meditation enables an individual to conclude that there is really nothing happen-

33. *Middle Length Sayings (Majjhima-Nikāya)*, vol. 1, p. 59.

ing in the world but such fresh disclosures. Most of these, however, get caught in our linguistic nets so effectively that they are no longer a discernible part of conscious thought. By teaching us to analyze this intellectual imagery, meditation facilitates a readiness to look for those new approaches to our problems which an existing body of reliable knowledge often prevents everyone from seeing.

Nowhere does human life display its underdeveloped and unfinished state more dramatically than in the way language systems gloss over the real centers of experience in favor of gross tactics and conceptions that resist further analysis and dislodgement. The living centers of experience, where fresh qualities are forever enriching life, go uncared for, callously ignored because conventional forms of thought leave these moments out of account. The meaning and quality are emerging so swiftly at these centers of awareness—these fleeting instants—that they slip through the linguistic filters of ordinary life and call for special analyses and perceptions if they are to be reinstated and enjoyed. No one notices their swift cumulations of aesthetic richness that run like a refreshing spring in the nerve endings and neural networks of all sensate experience. Our holiest contact with life, the fleeting instants themselves, are either forgotten or given over into the common medium of exchange, sometimes from an imperious need to conform.[34]

There are moments in Buddhist meditation—the method of freedom—when all distractions and socially coercive conceptual structures vanish, and the pure experience of life's qualitative flow wins the sole claim on attention. People capable of such moments experience the peace that literally surpasses all understanding. Even more, these are the great self-enjoyed syntheses experienced in the turmoil of contemporary life, amid days of tension and stress. We are then acting in accordance with our deepest and most creative nature, and we are for the moment free.

The Buddha nowhere appears to have said that such free-

34. See W. C. Macomber, *The Anatomy of Disillusion*, pp. 8ff., 74, 81.

dom in this life lasts forever. "The compassionate Buddha," as he has always been known, was probably incapable of believing that people are fools who suffer the bondage of the self and its compulsive striving. His analysis is effective in stopping the internal dialogue from its incessant reign over experience, and the penetrations that follow into the very heart of existence place suffering at least in a state of remission. There are reasons, at least, for believing that no claim for a permanent and absolute cure can be based upon the Buddha's teachings. The interminable speculations among his followers as to what happened to him when he died are persuasive evidence of this point. However, the daily lives of quiet desperation in compulsive striving may be reversed and overcome when the drivenness of insatiable needs, of wanting what life can never yield—security against disease and death, unlimited abundance for everyone through ever-new technological revolutions, safety from attack by more powerful persons and nations, defense against the pain of powerlessness and deprivation, and craving for logically valid and verifiable beliefs to save us from despair in the face of the unpredictable character and magnitude of the world—have been brought to an end in the Copernican Revolution that occurs in the depths when an individual truly awakens to the unutterable wonder of being alive.

There are forty meditations in the Theravāda tradition alone, among which are the Sublime States: (1) mettā ("good will") for all living beings without discrimination, (2) karunā ("compassion") for all living beings in trouble and affliction, (3) muditā ("sympathetic joy") in the success of others, and (4) upekkhā ("equanimity") in all vicissitudes of life. To practice mettā illustrates how analysis and penetration go hand in hand. Mettā is defined by Narada Thera as "that which softens one's heart. Its direct enemy is attachment . . . and its indirect enemy is callousness. The culmination of mettā is the identification of oneself with all that is alive."[35] Starting with one's self and moving to loved ones, then returning to center and moving

35. Narada Thera, A Manual of Abhidhamma, pp. 125–127.

from self to people disliked and eventually to enemies, one discovers after a few weeks the attitude of uncaring and the built-in barriers to human-heartedness that are deep-rooted in the contemporary world. "May I (they) be well and happy; may I (they) be free from suffering and anxiety; may I (they) attain Nirvana." Another version of this call to the caring heart may be phrased: "May I (they) be well and happy; may the passing moment be experienced in its fullness, without distraction, anxiety, and want; may I (they) experience the vivid flow of quality driving on to novelty forever." When persisted in for half an hour in perfect relaxation over a period of some weeks or months, the results of such meditation begin to emerge in striking new patterns of awareness and freedom.

The varieties of meditation are for different somatotypes and dispositions. An individual who sees faults everywhere, who may be driven by perfection, may find opportunities to attend to what is truly beautiful, to a color in all its radiance and brilliance,[36] while a person dominated by a general possessiveness, or by a proprietary mind, may be able to emerge from such compulsions by attending to what is ugly, to a color that is repulsive to him, or even by contemplating in a cemetery the decaying remains of one who was the picture of health.

Only as meditation yields results such as these does an individual become free from the powers that veil creativity everywhere in life. Only with success in digging up the wrong motivations formed around the roots of character does a person become capable of constructive action in the parliaments, the professions, and the welfare agencies of the contemporary world. Programs presently in place, because they are enacted by self-serving bureaucracies, have persuaded millions of compassionate people that something new must be explored. A large part of social reconstruction hinges upon whether men and women of the contemporary world can extinguish the fires that operate compulsively within themselves. This is why Nishitani comments that the present widespread confidence

36. Herbert V. Guenther, *Philosophy and Psychology in the Abhidharma*, pp. 137–138.

that what is pathological in the present age can be cured by political action "is not an insignificant part of the crisis itself."[37]

The precarious hold the present world has over its humanity is often revealed in the bizarre unwillingness members of different racial and ethnic groups display at any suggestion that meditation could open them for more creative participation in their confrontations with one another. Too distracted by leadership drives to give undivided attention to questions regarding their own cultural encapsulation in doctrinaire positions, they appear strangely disoriented from the freedom they profess to seek in the creative continuum of life. Many have forgotten that their deepest personal hunger is for direct experience of life responding to life. They have then lost the ability to distinguish what is alive from what is dead and dying. The number of people is not small who are capable of deliberately and consciously willing the destruction of civilized life in any form. They constitute the ground floor in the contemporary world from which tyranny and terrorism arise, and they personify the growing emphasis on methods of coercion and military might. In the face of the growing gulf between the rich and the poor in every metropolitan center of the world, the size of the police force, equipped and trained in more and more lethal weapons, must grow to deal with the looting that results when the lights go out. It is not strange that all nations of the contemporary world spent two and one-half times as much for military weapons as they spent in a typical recent year (1976) on public health. Two nations whose identity none would question accounted for fifty-four per cent of the $400 billion for arms. One of the best kept secrets of the most powerful civilization in history—the West—is the barbaric fact that violence has been the primary mode of sustaining its own large-scale existence. At the pinnacle of its vast concentration of wealth, it presently encounters the hardest threshold in the entire human career: the threshold with the question of how this wealth can provide conditions that foster the aesthetic enrichment and the widening range

37. Keiji Nishitani, "The Awakening of Self in Buddhism," p. 3.

of awareness of everyone on earth. Only through the rigors of meditation, perhaps, does anyone recognize that this is the question that distinguishes life from the dead and dying. And it enables us to see the immediate and pressing relevance of "The Self-Corrective Buddhist Way."

6

$\sim\sim\sim\sim\sim\sim\sim\sim\sim\sim\sim\sim\sim\sim\sim\sim\sim\sim\sim$

The Self-Corrective Buddhist Way

In the history of Buddhism, there have been no disputes between religious beliefs and scientific knowledge, since Buddhism is not contradictory to science. There is no point at which science comes into conflict with Buddhism, which is fully in accord with reason. Buddhism does not ask its followers to believe in anything outside the normal order of nature. Thus the rationality of Buddhism is required most in our age. Einstein himself wrote that if there is any religion which is acceptable to the modern scientific mind, it is Buddhism, because it applies to all times and to all men without regard to race, nation, or faith.

> *Chamnong Tongprasert*
> *Royal Institute*
> *Bangkok, Thailand*

FOUR OR FIVE MILLION years ago, in places like Olduvai Gorge, the first beginnings were made in the long and tortuous effort of the species to survive. Ten thousand years ago, in the great estuaries and riverine regions of the major continents, the creatures with the human future in their gene pool were discovering new techniques of agriculture and social organization with which to lift themselves from a hunting and gathering way of life into the new life styles of civilization. This was the first fundamental change after the initial emergence of our species. Ten thousand years in the greenhouses of civilization have brought us to the third great transmutation. The windows in the greenhouses are broken. The linguistic and behavioral incubators of relatively closed culture-worlds are falling into fragments as global changes sweep them together in an interdependent world. Several decades of global interaction between culture-worlds radically different from each other have already deposited in the experience of millions an awareness that, despite the multiform routines by which they are expected to live, they are all members of an amorphous global community into which, as Toynbee observed a quarter century ago, "the whole habitable world has now been unified."[1]

For the first time in history men and women are being emancipated from social coercions and forms of rigidity that ruled all but the most exceptional individuals until now. Individuals hitherto had little or no choice but to remain for life within the thought-world in which they were born; they now pass from one geographical area to another and exercise discretion and control over the values that give meaning to their lives. Many millions feel more at home among people on the opposite side of the world than among those with whom they had been reared. Such experiences alter in a radical way humankind's relation to the earth.

Life begins now more fully and freely to respond to life, creating a global civilization vitalized with innovation and self-correction beyond anything humankind has even dreamed. Freedom from parochialisms of race, creed, social class, peer group, and ethnic tradition is moving millions of men and women into a new appreciation of life—in one another, in the deepest reaches of the atmosphere, in the earth's tender crust, in the deepest levels of the sea. The grip of ancestral myth has been broken, releasing a mental and emotional maganimity and a freedom from visual and intellectual clichés. They are presently gathering the needed momentum to move the polarized conflicts of nations and ideologies to the back of the international stage. They are assimilating to the life they share with one another a more imaginative appraisal of what it means to be alive.

1. Arnold J. Toynbee, *Civilization on Trial*, p. 159.

The appearance of these emancipated men and women is still an exception rather than the rule. The vast majority can even now be mobilized into giving their time and substance to exclusively local concerns. But as the emancipated grow in numbers relative to the population at large, they bear witness to an intrinsically mysterious and aesthetically breathtaking, compassionate world. And they sense the presence of new possibilities for bringing the vast powers of modern science under commitment to the spontaneous qualities of life itself.

The growing community of this more deeply humanized population has already brought to the forefront of awareness the secret that has lived in obscurity, the knowledge that men and women have the capacity for becoming *self-corrective*, for changing the way they have been reared, for rethinking from time to time everything they have concluded regarding the dynamic and beautiful universe of which their living is a part. Their main problem may now be to make their mistakes as rapidly as possible and move together out of those special and exclusive interests which socially fragmented communities of the superindustrial age tend to endow with a life and purpose of their own.

Human life has made spectacular shifts onto new plateaus during its long evolutionary past, but never on a global scale. Failure to carry out self-corrective adaptation may have brought hundreds of side branches of human evolution to the end of their line of development, as in the case of the Neanderthal people who appear in the fossil record of our prehistoric past between one hundred thousand and thirty-five thousand years ago. Survival in our time is a challenge which can be met only by the human community as a geographical and cultural unit, utilizing in an all-sided way the self-corrective capabilities that nurtured our long evolution. Just as we all share a common origin among the *Homo* ancestors of the distant past, we now share inescapably a common destiny, a destiny, as Richard Leakey and Roger Lewin state, "that the human race is now capable of choosing."[2] Ironically enough, it

2. Richard Leakey and Roger Lewin, *People of the Lake*, p. 282.

is a destiny to be determined by unprecedented penetrations of the mind, powerful enough to devise ways of destroying the entire adventure nature has been making in humankind, and also powerful and perceptive enough to render obsolete the lethal ways of war.

The issue of survival serves to single out for the attention of all humanity the two clearly defined communities where the greatest joys of life have been associated with the process of self-correction. One of these is the community of modern science. The other is the venerable Buddhist legacy, where self-correction has operated on the most personal level for twenty-five hundred years.

Creative continuance of the human adventure may depend upon the fresh perceptions each of these self-corrective communities can acquire from one another. This possibility has not gone without recognition by leaders of the two traditions. Hartshorne has recently remarked that "Buddhism and modern science are very likely the two most fully self-corrective communities we know," and the leading exemplar of the Theravāda legacy, Nyānaponika Mahāthera, has made the same observation. "No one should be the least hesitant," Nyānaponika writes, "to place in juxtaposition (1) the Buddha's self-corrective method, and (2) the exemplification of it in the scientific community (though limited and imperfect)." Others have made similar remarks, among them Henry Margenau: "Buddhist ethics have been amazingly effective, and they display almost in pure culture the characteristics of a system patterned after science."[3]

The present threat to the continuance of life on the planet is the result of the inability of contemporary humanity to bring these two self-corrective legacies together in relations of mutual understanding and support. Nothing in the character of either one stands unyielding in the way of their collaboration "for the welfare of the many," to use the Buddha's phrase, except the narrow limits of their understanding of one an-

3. Both the Hartshorne and Nyānaponika quotes are from personal communication with author; Henry Margenau, *Ethics and Science*, p. 255.

other, their failure to appreciate how much they may have in common, and certain obstacles of personal prejudice and cultural bias which are scarcely the exclusive feature of any community we know. Their ignorance of each other results from the failure of both to comprehend a type of behavior that seems to be radically different from their own. If their cultural encapsulation can be brought to an end, they may be seen as the Yin and Yang of the organized self-corrective community of tomorrow.

THE CULTURAL DISINTEGRATION OF MODERN SCIENCE

Nothing is more strange about the modern era than the surprising speed with which the institutions of the special sciences have been swallowed up by the traditional culture-world they were from the very beginning seeking to transform. Wearied by the fierce struggles of the Reformation, the Counter-Reformation, the Spanish Inquisition, and the Wars of Religion (1560–1648), Europeans saw in science a new promise, enunciated by Sir Francis Bacon in 1605 as "for the glory of the Creator and the relief of man's estate,"[4] and more specifically as an agency capable of lifting humanity's vision from stupefying toil, from a life "brutish and brief" onto horizons free from drudgery and privation, ignorance and disease, tyranny and oppression. All impediments to which spirit and flesh are heir were expected to find their resolution in science. Science would provide the social foundations upon which more democratic ways of life could grow, where people would enjoy a common future in fathoming everything, trying everything, extending everything, wondering, doubting, testing, giving their lives to widen the range of what can be seen, known, experienced, and done. A new view of truth lay at the heart of the scientific revolution from the beginning: truth is a belief whose limitations have not yet been disclosed. Through open discussion and communication of the results of scientific investigation, every person's beliefs and doubts would

4. Quoted in R. Hooykas, "Science and Reformation," p. 265.

eventually stand corrected; the incorrigible mind would be changed without resorting to the methods of the Inquisition.

As recently as twenty years ago, C. P. Snow could describe this culture of modern science as the wave of the future. Snow said in his May 1959 Rede Lecture at Cambridge:

> The scientific culture really is a culture, not only in an intellectual but also in an anthropological sense. That is, its members need not, and of course often do not, always completely understand each other, but there are common attitudes, common standards and patterns of behavior, common approaches and assumptions. This goes surprisingly wide and deep. It cuts across other mental patterns, such as those of religion or politics or class. In their working, and in much of their emotional life, their attitudes are closer to other scientists than to non-scientists who in religion or politics or class have the same labels as themselves. Without thinking about it, they respond alike. This is what a culture means.[5]

Whether born and reared as Christians, as in the case of Arthur Compton, or as a materialist, as J. D. Bernal; whether born rich, like Thomas Merton and Victor Rothschild, or born poor, as Ernest Rutherford, who was the son of an odd job handyman: they nonetheless are the carriers of a new culture of humankind—the scientific culture. Individual scientists can remain widely and deeply open and perceptive in the midst of failure and breakdown of everything heretofore considered sound and established in their special science. Creativity is prized over temporary success. Error, especially when clear and unambiguous, is highly productive in the scientific culture. More important than the scientific community, with its fund of reliable knowledge, is the process of self-corrective inquiry in which its members share across all social, racial, class and national lines. Together, they take account of the conditions responsible for their successes and failures and with a voracious appetite for new discovery move outward to include wider ranges of experience. No assumption is shared regarding the purpose of correcting what they know; the purpose is obvious to all. They are freer than most people of ra-

5. C. P. Snow, *The Two Cultures and the Scientific Revolution*, pp. 10–11.

cial feelings, and inclined to think that something problematic can be solved, until it is proved otherwise. They are not members of a creed in competition with other creeds. Jacob Bronowski described what he called "the stable society of science" in the decade following World War II. "No one," he wrote, "has been shot or exiled or convicted of perjury, no one has recanted abjectly at a trial before his colleagues. The whole structure of science has been changed, and no one has been either disgraced or deposed. Through all the changes of science, the society of scientists is flexible and single-minded together and evolves and rights itself. In the language of science, it is a stable society."[6]

Science conflicted with the traditional world in which it was born in ways that can be illustrated best in the work of Albert Einstein. He set out to criticize prevailing theories of space and time when experiments conducted in the framework of such theories suggested some need for modification. In one of the consummatory achievements of modern science, he developed a theory of relativity which has had powerful implications far beyond the original area of investigation. He displayed in this achievement the power to question and revise even the assumptive form-world of space and time, hitherto held as a necessary presupposition underlying all that was known about nature. No other influence has affected twentieth-century thought more deeply than Einstein's discovery of relativity. Henceforth, the observer must be considered along with his observations, since all knowledge is conditioned by the standpoint of the knower. Not even the theory of evolution has had such reverberations through the modern world as the discovery of spatial and temporal relativity. As Henry Stapp has put it, no experience can be isolated from its connections with the totality of things.[7]

Another dramatic way of illustrating the remarkable integ-

6. Jacob Bronowski, *Science and Human Values*, p. 82.

7. Henry Peirce Stapp, "S-Matrix Interpretation of Quantum Theory," pp. 303–320. See also Gary Zukav, *The Dancing Wu Li Masters*, pp. 277, 284; also Fritjof Capra, *The Tao of Physics*, pp. 24–25, 68–69, 80–81, and 285–307.

rity and stability of the culture of science is to observe its vitality and resilience in the face of revolutionary changes in prevailing belief. Max Born, Nobel Prize winner in 1954, has left us his personal testimony regarding the changes in his own field of investigation:

> In 1921 I believed—and I shared this belief with most of my contemporary physicists—that science produced an objective knowledge of the world, which is governed by deterministic laws. In 1951 I believed in none of these things. The border between object and subject had been blurred, deterministic laws had been replaced by statistical ones, and although physicists understood one another well enough across all national frontiers they had contributed nothing to a better understanding of nations, but had helped in inventing and applying the most horrible weapons of destruction. Even the firm tapestry of nature itself had lost its substantial character in the opening decades of the present century.[8]

Bronowski makes the same point. "There is today," he writes, "almost no scientific theory which was held when, say the Industrial Revolution began about 1760. Most often today's theories flatly contradict those of 1760; many contradict those of 1900. In cosmology, in quantum mechanics, in genetics, in the social sciences, who now holds the beliefs that seemed firm fifty years ago? Yet the society of scientists has survived these changes without a revolution and honors the men whose beliefs it no longer shares."[9]

Students of modern science trace this stability of their society to the method or methods they employ. As Ernest Nagel puts it, "The history of science cannot but appear as a catalogue of error, without a competent understanding of the method of science. Apart from such understanding, one set of dogmatic claims to truth seems to be replaced by another set no less precarious, and every change is then judged as fresh evidence for the 'bankruptcy' of science and for the incapacity of the human mind to attain genuine knowledge by way of scientific inquiry."[10] Nothing could reflect more adequately this

8. Max Born, *My Life and My Views*, pp. 190–191.
9. Bronowski, *Science and Human Values*, p. 86.
10. Ernest Nagel, "The Place of Science in a Liberal Education," p. 60.

emphasis upon the methodology of science than the widely circulated report, bearing the title "The Integrity of Science," released by the Board of Directors of the American Association for the Advancement of Science in 1964:

The ultimate source of the strength of science will not be found in its impressive products or in its powerful instruments. It will be found in the minds of the scientists, and in the system of discourse which scientists have developed in order to describe what they know and to perfect their understanding of what they have learned. It is these internal factors—the methods, procedures, and processes which scientists use to discover and to discuss the properties of the natural world—which have given science its great success.

Such are the major ingredients of the culture of modern science that came to prominence with Copernicus and Galileo, achieved formal organization in the various Royal Academies of England, France, and the rest of the Western world, and proceeded to rise to dominance until (and including) World War II. All scientists, regardless of race, religion, social class, ethnic or national tradition shared together a common culture. Biologists, chemists, astronomers, geneticists, oceanographers, high energy physicists—all shared a common methodology, yet something deeper than methods. All shared common attitudes, assumptions, expectations, as they sifted, refined, and corrected even the presuppositions with which inquiry began.

Confining ourselves to the way scientists have thought about the culture they shared we see a process of inquiry that grows stronger, rather than weaker, in the face of error and radical criticism—even falsification—of existing scientific belief. Flexibility in creating new theoretical models is what science is all about, whether in biology, mathematics, or geology. All the sciences have this major qualification for belonging: the capacity for imagining some new theory that enables one to perceive evidence previously hidden by existing beliefs. The community of inquiry has this central feature: individual members are free to offer new evidence with the assumption that no one will be unable to accept the possibility that they have been wrong. This requires that individual scientists will be honest in dealing with available evidence. No other enterprise appears to have this feature of honesty, trust, and mutual reinforcement—not even the life of intimate lovers. As felt and understood by its own members, the culture of modern science was borne along by the deep-running tides of reality, while all around the culture there existed in the lives of nonscientists those other methods of custom, supernatural revelation, personal threat and coercion by which people were controlled in whatever they thought. The culture of modern science represented a radically new technique for coordinating what men and women shall conclude without coercion. If there were a victory of this culture over the traditional one in which it was somehow spawned from about 1600 up to and including World War II, the acquisitive society would be forced to retire from the center of the historical stage, yielding the stage to an expanding community of experience, cooperation, and self-correction and sharing. This would indeed be a revolutionary change in the deep-running tide, turning over the direction of the vessel of human history to *Homo correctus*, whose deepest nature is to inquire, to observe, to attend, to awaken, and to alter his behavior in the light of what *Homo sapiens*, *Homo faber*, and *Homo symbolicum* had been incapable of perceiving. Men and women would inscribe upon their banners the new motto of the Royal Society, *Nullius in Verba* ("Take nobody's word for it; see for yourself").

The major function of the culture of modern science, it now seems clear, has been to liberate humankind from the conventional, custom-bound ways of the traditional cultures in which it has been maturing for several centuries. One of the most dramatic features of the story of its deepening disclosures, Nicholas Maxwell observes, "is the long painful way in which highly parochial, egocentric, anthropomorphic ideas have been made a little less parochial, a little less egocentric and anthropomorphic. Thus the search for standards of intelligibility which are as unparochial as possible, which can be appreciated by the widest possible range of possible beings, and not merely by human beings from a particular culture, is a fundamental feature of the development of scientific knowledge." Maxwell then quotes John Archibald Wheeler's clear perception of a "universe that is far stranger and more beautiful than we realize," but a universe we have no hope of seeing in its simplicity and beauty "until we first realize how strange it is."[11]

Throughout the history of modern science, explorers have been crippled in their imagination by the almost hypnotic grip of provincialism, ethnocentricity, and narrow nationalism, all of which threaten to reach pathological forms in the contemporary scene. An entirely natural inertia of human thought makes individuals reluctant to introduce new assumptions and even more reluctant to change the total intellectual perspective. Few of Darwin's contemporaries, for example, including his close friend Charles Lyell, were able to agree with his evolutionary theory because that would have required them to rethink everything they considered true. The chief reason why the theory of evolution has made such slow progress both during and after Darwin's time is that it has required a shift to an entirely new world view directly in conflict with traditional systems of belief.[12]

The natural inertia of thought has been an adversary of sufficient strength to slow the progress of science and give critical holding power to the traditional culture, particularly during the volatile changes introduced by quantum physics, relativity theory, and genetics during the twentieth century. The drag of tradition has recently been reinforced by an even more powerful adversary to the culture of modern science— the captivity of all free self-corrective inquiry on an organized scale to the power establishment which during World War II earned the title of "the military-industrial complex." The most famous warning probably came from President Eisenhower as he left office three days before the inauguration of John Fitzgerald Kennedy. The speech had been in the making for

11. Nicholas Maxwell, "The Rationality of Scientific Discovery," p. 271.
12. See Ernst Mayr, "The Nature of the Darwinian Revolution."

almost two years, so concerned was the President to say something comparable to George Washington's famous "Farewell Address."

In the councils of government [Eisenhower warned] we must guard against the acquisition of unwarranted influence, whether sought or unsought, by the military-industrial complex. The potential for the disastrous rise of misplaced power exists and will persist. We must never let the weight of this combination endanger our liberties or democratic processes. We should take nothing for granted. Only an alert and knowledgeable citizenry can compel the proper meshing of the huge industrial and military machinery of defense with our peaceful methods and goals so that security and liberty may prosper together.[13]

One leading physicist, Max Born, sees the objectivity of science as having been destroyed by science itself. "In the operation of science and its ethics," he writes, "a change has taken place that makes it impossible to maintain the old ideal of the pursuit of knowledge for its own sake which my generation believed in. We were convinced that this could never lead to any evil since the search for truth was good in itself. That was a beautiful dream from which we were awakened by world events. Even the deepest sleepers awoke when, in August 1945, the first atom bombs fell on Japanese cities."[14]

All of the most fully industrialized nations of the contemporary world exercise essentially the same control over the culture of science. In a world where fear and aggression dominate the relations between nations, the scientist motivated by the self-corrective quest is always under close surveillance by the military-industrial complex, as Eisenhower's speech suggests. The treatment accorded Robert Oppenheimer in his public trial and humiliation is only matched in history by that of his famous predecessor, Galilei Galileo.[15] There is pathos in the cable sent by the United States Academy of Sciences in

13. Quoted in Robert J. Donovan, Washington Post-Los Angeles Times News Service, "The Origin of Ike's Most Quoted Line," *The Charlotte Observer*, April 7, 1969.
14. Max Born, *My Life and My Views*, pp. 190–191.
15. See G. de Santillana, *Reflections on Men and Ideas*.

1973 to their opposite unit, the Soviet Academy of Sciences, seeking support and protection for Andrei Sakharov, father of Russia's hydrogen bomb, in the face of political persecution from which the American group had been unable to protect their own Oppenheimer following World War II.[16]

Budgetary statistics remove all doubt that the culture of science has met in the military-industrial complex the agency capable of bringing to an end the momentum science had acquired until World War II for transforming the traditional culture-world of which it is a part. With $22 billion budgeted for research and development in 1977 by the United States alone, supplemented by $18 billion from the business sector and foundations, as compared to total expenditures of $166 million in 1930, and just over $5 billion in 1953, we see an acceleration of expenditure for "Big Science" which would exceed the entire gross national product by the end of this century if it continued rising at almost the same rate. The figures are precisely the same in this respect in Russia.

The tremendous cost of the facilities required in modern science brings all members as fully under control by the power elite as Archimedes in the famous testing of the gold in King Hiero's crown. Projects that can be translated almost immediately into new engines of destruction have brought greater increase in the GNP than the whole of humanity achieved in all history up to the beginning of the present decade. With each percentage point, the pollution of the soil with lethal chemicals grows without detection until entire neighborhoods have experienced abnormal births, deaths, and incurable diseases over a period that may last several decades before they are even linked with industrial waste.

It is difficult to imagine a more relentless self-destructive trend than the one into which humankind appears presently to be locked and bolted by the two belligerents—the United States and the Soviet Union—who think of themselves as adversaries, but for the time being are dragging the entire human community in the same direction. A world no longer

16. See *Science* 181 (1973): 1148–1149.

manageable within the limits of the most widespread assumptions and compulsive drives—security, a predictable tomorrow, freedom to acquire all attainable wealth and power—is being coerced by the very challenge of survival to seek out new angles of perception in which the planet's present plight might be corrected. Under such conditions, the nation or civilization that cannot penetrate its inflexible designs for living rushes obliviously into irretrievable disaster.

At the same time, it should be conceded that evidence appears to be overwhelming that the redirection of the prevailing course of human development does not lie within the competence of those most responsible for the present trend. Men and women living under the circumstances of the superindustrial age, according to Erich Fromm, are rarely aware of the mechanization of their own subjective existence. People living in such a system, Fromm writes, "become indifferent to life and even attracted to death." They become, Fromm continues, "indifferent to life, fascinated by the mechanical, and eventually attracted by death and total destruction."[17] The capacity men and women have for experiencing joy in the unrepeatable now, and for celebrating the wonder of being alive, has suffered setbacks which may be irreversible under the conditions of the contemporary world.

The secret of the creativity that is life's ultimate source of meaning and renewal is well hidden from all whose lives are caught in the institutionalized behavior of the superindustrial age. The valuing consciousness of these people, their angles of perception, the mental habits acquired since they were young, and the pressures of social conformity which few seem able to resist—all wind like the convoluted pathways of a modern labyrinth around the tenderness of life itself, subjecting everything and everyone to the senseless compulsions of a pathological world. This modern labyrinth expresses itself in the anthropological view of culture as having an independent reality of its own, apart from the energizing centers of life. Lost in this labyrinth, men and women appear to acquire

17. Erich Fromm, *The Heart of Man*, pp. 59, 58.

their conclusions about their own experience as did the dwellers of Plato's allegory of the cave. Sealed off—like the isolationist Japan of the Tokugawa period—from vital contact with life's vivid qualitative flow, such people harbor forms of understanding that throw the really growing world in as deep a darkness as the other side of the moon. The most dangerous people in the present world are these, for they are incapable of self-correction, having permitted their culture-world to exercise its imperious control over the soft underside of their lives.

THE OTHER SELF-CORRECTIVE COMMUNITY

The point that may confer added momentum to the Buddhist encounter with the community of modern science is that self-corrective powers have been operating in the experience of men and women of Buddhist persuasion for twenty-five centuries. In comparison, the community of modern science offers at best several centuries of exceptional achievement which loosened the compulsive grip of traditional views of man and nature, only to have its own center of gravity shattered by the superior power of war.

As different as Buddhism and modern science may seem, they are in some important respects alike. Both have considerable power to shift the conduct of life *away from* established beliefs, however reliable and legitimate, *over to* the self-corrective mode of behavior. Both are alert to what Wittgenstein called "the bewitchment of the intellect by language." As we have had occasion to observe, Buddhism is considerably freer in this respect. Both are problem centered, again with the same difference—Buddhism everywhere has been known for its pragmatic bent, for addressing questions to which some conceivable experience might provide answers. Buddhism has always insisted that it is a form of practical-critical activity, rather than a textbook of theory, just as science asserts with complete candor that its history is littered with the dry bones of one-time well-attested beliefs. Both, therefore, predispose their members to rethink from time to time everything they have been reared to believe, and there is no inducement in all this for members to fall into cynicism and despair. The pragmatic bent of Buddhism is seen particularly in the parable of the arrow, where speculation over unanswerable questions is discouraged in the face of the need for alleviating the suffering of the person who has been wounded; and, likewise, in the parable of the raft, in which a man finds materials to build a raft to cross the river, then throws the raft away instead of walking about for the rest of his life as though with some saving doctrine on his back.

Until field work by anthropologists provided evidence to the contrary,[18] Buddhism was widely viewed as opposed to modernization—that metamorphosis of self-correction operating in individual and community to correct the torrent of uncriticized and obsolete power structures in South and Southeast Asia. Modernization was an opportunity everywhere in Burma, Sri Lanka, and Thailand for exploring a new identity for Buddhism, especially in places emerging into freedom from British colonial rule. Public officials, monks, and Buddhist laypeople in Rangoon met weekly in dozens of groups to explore resources for achieving that new identity. Modernizing elites, often educated in the West, were slow in discovering the role Buddhist leadership was prepared to play in releasing their people from the prevailing culture-bound condition.[19] What distinguishes Buddhism in this respect, in part, is its own unequivocally egalitarian and democratic life, its freedom from presumptions of authority of person over person, and, on the other hand, its focus upon improvement *from within* through meditation. A parable from the Pali texts illustrates that modernity and tradition were not mutually exclusive in the ancient Theravāda background:

Two men go out in search of treasure, come across a heap of hemp thrown away, bundle it up, and go ahead. On the way they come

18. Arthur Niehoff, "Theravāda Buddhism: A Vehicle for Technical Change," pp. 108–112. Cf. P. M. Prayudha Payutto, "Problems, Status and Duties of the Sangha in Modern Society."
19. See Soedjatmoko, "Cultural Motivations to Progress."

across hempen thread, hempen cloth, a heap of linen thread, linen cloth, cotton down, cotton thread and calico, iron, copper, tin, lead, silver and gold. At each stage the progressive person makes his change for the better item, while the conservative person retains his bundle of hemp, saying, "I've brought this load of hemp a long way, Friend, and it's well tied up; that's enough for me; you choose for yourself." Ultimately, the progressive person who came back with gold found pleasure and happiness and was praised by his friends and relations, while the other is condemned for his foolish beliefs, which were a source of sorrow to him.[20]

It has been difficult to dislodge from the uninformed "modernizers" of the West the prejudice that Buddhism has not been interested in the improvement of life, not to mention outright revolution.[21] Much confusion would have been forestalled if the distinctions had been kept clearly in mind from the start between westernization by the forward stampede and the perfectibility of life to which Buddhism has always been committed. The widespread persuasion that some kind of political act, apart from individual experiential enrichment, can produce a wholesale emancipation is not an insignificant part of the crisis of the superindustrial age. From a Buddhist perspective, it can be taken as a truism that the fate of humanity, and perhaps of all but the most elementary forms of life on the planet, rests firmly upon the ability ordinary men and women can now develop for breaking the strands of compulsive behavior and choosing the path of emancipation and purification.

Where Buddhism differs from what C. P. Snow referred to as the culture of modern science is in their ways of viewing the correction and enrichment of life, and here they may eventually be seen to supplement much more than to contradict each other. What truly separates the two major self-corrective communities of the contemporary world is the Buddhist perception that life everywhere is self-enjoyed and capable of acquiring its own creative meaning and value in the

20. *Dialogues of the Buddha (Dīgha-Nikāya)*, part 2, pp. 369–370.
21. See R. Puligandla and K. Puhakka, "Buddhism and Revolution." In China, Buddhism was frequently at the center of peasant rebellions from the thirteenth century on.

fleeting moment of one's life. This persuasion expresses itself, as we have seen, in the central conception of *pratitya-samut-pada* ("creative origination"), in the diagnosis and cure for suffering, in the orientation and method of human freedom, and in the consummatory experience of Nirvana. Efforts to bring the most intimate dimensions of life into harmony with the world's creative qualitative flow predispose Buddhism to reject all dualisms with which non-Buddhist societies gener-ally are afflicted—man and nature, God (or Allah) and the world, life and death, mind and body, fact and value, change and permanence, and many others indicated in chapter 3. For Buddhism, there is no background of sanctified categories and values upon which members of any culture-world may fall back. Human experience is *experienced* as continuous with the rest of nature. By rigorous struggle and discipline, any individual can be freed from the entire linguistic system of categories and values of a bifurcating culture, both sacred and profane.

Judgments concerned with the internal, intimate, and in-tensely personal domain of a bifurcating self in a bifurcating world are conceived in modern science, on the contrary, as lying outside the scope of critical investigation. Such matters are "subjective," because they belong to a subject who, ex-cept in the investigations of Capra and Henry Stapp, is not an organic part of the "objective" world. Unlike members of the Buddhist self-corrective Way, modern scientists, with the rare exception of an occasional Einstein, borrow their atti-tudes and values on these matters, more or less like school-boys, from the ancestral order and tradition that lie outside their narrow specialization. Like those of whom Søren Kier-kegaard was thinking in his famous aphorism,[22] they accept the assumptions of the culture-world in which they were reared. Members of the self-corrective culture of modern science, therefore, devote all personal knowledge and discovery to matters that exclude the intimate and internal concerns, with

22. "There are many people who reach their conclusions about life like schoolboys; they cheat their master by copying the answer out of a book without having worked out the sum for themselves." *The Journals of Søren Kierkegaard*, p. 39.

the result that their judgments regarding freedom and suffering resemble in all major respects the judgments of any other member of their social class and tradition.

Buddhism has always been persuaded that life is one, self-corrective, and self-surpassing, and Buddhism's methods of meditation and analysis are designed to free men and women from the self-serving, time-bound, authoritarian social institutions that now threaten the adventure nature has been making in man. Modern science, on the contrary, first emerged and has continued to flourish in culture-worlds where questions about the ultimate form of the world and its possibilities for human value have been exhaustively determined for all time. This is the predicament that bars modern science effectively from modifying those compulsive drives and values in defense of which nations of the superindustrial age are constantly improving their capability for nuclear war. The most highly developed methods of scientific research afford their exemplars no observation that might slow the headlong momentum of war. By their silence and personal detachment, perhaps, modern scientists are often perceived by their countrymen as sources of assurance regarding the validity of the structures each rising generation is asked to defend.

Buddhism rejects the dismal picture of the ego-centered, culture-encapsulated life, offering in its place a deepening individuality capable of clearing up the self-torture of men and women who must remain separate, isolated, and insoluble mysteries to one another and to themselves. This deepening individuality runs through the momentary self, but the self is numerically a new actuality each moment. Momentary selves may be thought of as egos, but the ego is not present for seventy years presiding over the fate of a single entity. The individual is always *here* in the passing now, free to enjoy life where it really is, and free to accept the universe in the aesthetic flow of the vivid present. From the vantage point of each numerically new momentary self, individuals are able to perceive how something earlier in the series may have been wrong, and they can participate in weaving together lives that are forever new.

To become more fully aware of the qualities alive in the passing now is to become more awakened to the very drive of the universe itself. Qualities of the moment can be synthesized to create ever more rich and deepening dimensions of life. Men and women are thus capable of becoming more creative participants in the lives they share with those who live, with those who have lived, and with those who will yet live.

The clearer we perceive this deepening individuality inherent in the Buddhist Way, the more opportunity we have for overcoming a radical inconsistency at the base of modern thought which accounts for much that is wavering and halfhearted in our civilization. Minds cleared of error-ridden, independent, nonidentical existences can *experience their own experience* in its concrete qualitative authenticity. Such minds are increasingly free to focus upon opportunities for selfcorrection as they engage their fellow-creatures in militant probing of vital issues always emerging on the troubled surface of the contemporary world.

Greater awareness is generated in this way both within and between our bodies, unclogging physiological processes from the cholesterol deposited by creeds, dogmas, ideologies, delusions, resentments, and all the other self-fulfilling justifications that gather as men and women grapple with the fundamental disorientation of their lives. To the measure that we can sustain the human system in openness from one moment to the next, we leap from our isolation, from our self-isolating cocoons, and we become one with the sources of the world's vitality and joy. As such individuality deepens and broadens, we discover that we touch one another for either life or death, and suddenly the whole world is where we are.

This is the self-corrective Buddhist Way which makes it possible literally to love the other as oneself, that is, as not another substance.[23] Buddhists have laws to assist people in ordering the serial moments of their careers, but their societies are bound together by personal relations rather than by law. A law professor from a major university in the United

23. See Charles Hartshorne, *The Logic of Perfection*, p. 122.

States was recently quoted as saying, "We are a legalistic society, and anyone seeking to change our behavior will be well advised to enter the legal profession." To change society for the better in the issue of human rights, for example, means to change the laws, to alter the rules in accordance with which people are expected to behave. Wherever Buddhism has been a major component of culture, on the contrary, society becomes better by changing the way people treat one another, and individuals are more socially effective than their legal systems. No law can take the fullness of concrete individuality into account, for the simple reason that the momentary actuality is forever creating what is real in the passing now and, therefore, what is necessarily the major source of personal and social change, whether for better or worse.

Freed from habitual obstructions, the Buddhist nonsubstantial self is in touch with the ultimate momentum of life; the fluctuations of fortune are not allowed to obscure the perpetual aesthetic creation of each moment. Attention is focused upon the concrete appeal of life for life, the fundamental drama being portrayed on this beautiful blue agate floating in the emptiness of space.

Govinda discusses the nonsubstantial self:

Instead of a world filled with dead things, there is a *living* cosmos which finds its counterpart in the consciousness of each individual and its focus in each atom, just as every moment from the standpoint of infinitesimal divisibility contains the boundlessness of time. Thus we find present *within* ourselves the eternity and abundance which are denied to us as long as we are seeking them in the phantasmagoria of an eternal world or of a separate little ego.[24]

The two distinctive self-corrective communities of the contemporary world are ultimately rooted, therefore, in a polar opposition much deeper than some to which we have referred. In Buddhism there is no determinate actuality at the center of existence; there is only a creativity infinitely productive of determinate events; each passing moment participates and

24. Lama Anagarika Govinda, *The Psychological Attitude of Early Buddhist Philosophy*, p. 142.

hence contributes to whatsoever is actualized in this world. The poorest man or woman plays a potentially creative role in the qualitative enrichment of unforeseen outcomes without which, in the interrelated world of the Buddhist perspective, there can be no experience and thus no reality at all. What is most rewarding, therefore, is never something aside from the usual activities of life. Man stands side by side with his fellows, sustained by the values they have nurtured in experience. As Yale's eminent professor of science and law, F. S. C. Northrop, has frequently suggested, the Buddhist Way provides the world with "the first, the largest, and the longest still-persisting egalitarian democratic social, political, religious, and familial communities this earth's surface has ever contained." Viewing the Buddha's Enlightenment as a momentous breakthrough, Northrop continues:

The Buddha not merely biologically observed, but also demonstrated behavioristically, initially with a bodily sensitive injured swan, that facing fellow-feelingfully shared pain and suffering, while also accepting pleasure when it is there *and fellow-feelingfully shared as good*, is not merely more biologically and psychologically realistic, but also a more naturally wise, aesthetically and religiously sensitive and *philo* of *sophic* way to face and live . . . the full temporal range of any living creature's existence, leaving one with a less soured and cynical disillusionment later on and a greater richer equanimity during the fall and winter of anyone's life, than does either (a) the focusing on merely introspectively psychic pleasure, even when added up statistically, or (b) the trusting in one's own, or anyone else's kinship anthropological genealogy of birth and culturally conditioned "law of status" familial, tribal and racist breeding. This is what makes the naturalistic realism of the compassionate Buddha unique even among Asians.[25]

Because self-correction is a responsibility resting naturally upon oneself, rather than upon "familial, tribal and racist lines of kinship," a Buddhist comes of age with an accumulation of experience out of which an emotively moving and compassionate community can be built.

25. F. S. C. Northrop, "Naturalistic Realism and Animate Compassion," pp. 182, 194.

A few self-corrective experiences that I had during my fieldwork in Rangoon clarified these observations forever. An argument between top officials of the city and a monastic population of perhaps 100,000 had developed over the question of what should be done in Oklappa, a suburb of 40,000 people, where malaria-infected mosquitos were threatening young and old, particularly since most houses had no screens. The controversy was everywhere, and it surfaced one day at the International Institute for Advanced Buddhistic Studies when a young English monk with a degree from Oxford took objection to the Western "solution" with which I had been reared.

"It is a simple case," I had remarked, "of who is to die, the mosquitos with DDT, or the children with malaria."

Looking at me intently, he objected, "You don't understand the point; it's not merely a question of killing mosquitos; it's a question of what happens to us when we kill."

As quickly as that, I have stood corrected during the intervening years. There is no countervailing evidence; killing affects the killer too, and it may leave its effects for a lifetime, even for many lives. This is why programs for alleviating and reclaiming the suffering of prisoners often commit in other forms what Karl Menninger has called "the crime of punishment." The British physicist, Jacob Bronowski, put the point in an almost Buddhist way: "We are all lonely. We've learnt to pity one another for being alone. And we've learnt that nothing remains to be discovered except compassion. At the end of years of despair, there is nothing to grow in you as tall as a blade of grass except your own humanity."[26] For a Buddhist, the compassion is discovered at the beginning, rather than at the end. Punishment is criminal because it marks the point at which an absolute separation occurs from the flow of unstructured quality that finds its natural voice in compassion.

The same personal relations all living creatures share together found frequent expression in the political squabbles of Rangoon. Thousands of homeless dogs were running in packs in the outskirts of the city, where monks fed them but could

26. Jacob Bronowski, *The Face of Violence*, pp. 161–162.

not stop the howling at all hours of the night; and people were afraid that dogs might attack them as they stood at bus stops munching sweets of one kind or another. Again the controversy emerged between city officials and the monks. No agreement could be reached until the officials agreed to put arsenic in only one of every six meatballs. This gave *karma* a chance to operate as a factor determining which dogs lived or died.

Through all such disagreements, no banner headlines joined the battle, setting one group against the other. Discussions were carried out in newspapers and over the radio, with all points of view being expressed in a rational way. People followed the controversies with fellow-feeling for the speechless world's living creatures. Discussions equally creative and self-corrective would be possible in all the assemblies of the world except for the prevailing threat to peace which ultimately stems from the more solidified positions people assume when they have laid down for them at birth their numerical, substantial identity—whether pigmented or white, rich or poor, hereditary nobility or middle class, Chicano or Vietnamese.

People whose identity can never be corrected because it was received at birth, rather than created in coming of age, constitute one of the enduring threats to the peace of the world, defending as they must their mutually independent nonidentical selves. They sometimes resort to sedatives to diminish the stress and achieve a brief period of peace among the warring members, but five billion doses of tranquilizers, three billion doses of amphetamines, and five billion doses of barbiturates *prescribed* yearly in the United States alone attest to the dark and enigmatic problem. To millions of such people, a large and lengthy war offers an avenue of escape from a confusing, insoluble problem.

The deeper polar opposition between Buddhism and modern science to which we have just alluded—the fact that in Buddhism there is no determinate actuality at the center of existence but only a creativity infinitely productive of determinate events—finds natural expression in the strong suspicion Buddhism has always harbored for conceptual systems and their institutionalization in cultural form. The concept, in the first place, threatens the organic unity of any individual's life, because it calls attention to itself and resists its assimilation into the organic wholeness of existence; born to throw light *into* the darkness, it tends to take the light *away from* the darkness. Secondly, theoretical models lend themselves to being held compulsively as instruments for advancing the self-isolating designs of the ego, sometimes to the point of becoming the principal barrier to fellow-feeling between people. Third, concepts provide every power structure, every dominant social class, every ethnic or racial establishment with its most effective means for the generalized control of behavior. Fourth, every idea offers itself as a possible pattern of avoidance, encouraging what has been called the ostrich-effect, where even the most valid proposition may commit perception to a tiny spectrum of life's rich qualitative flow. Finally, conceptual structures are almost universally torn from their contexts to become free-floating in doctrinaire ways, a problem that tortured Wittgenstein all his life, until he participated in the Gestalt-oriented reform of the Austrian school system under Karl Bühler in the 1920s, teaching for six years in village schools outside Vienna, where new experience—later presented in the *Investigations*—showed how language plays a *functional* role.

Whitehead's critique of science carries much the same objection to the danger inherent in conceptual systems. While the science of political economy immediately after Adam Smith destroyed many economic fallacies, Whitehead writes,

it did more harm than good. It riveted on men a certain set of abstractions which were disastrous in their influence on modern mentality. This is only one example of a general danger inherent in modern science. Its methodological procedure is exclusive and intolerant, and rightly so. It fixes attention on a definite group of abstractions, neglects everything else, and elicits every scrap of information and theory which is relevant to what it has retained. However triumphant, the triumph is within limits. The neglect of these limits leads to disastrous oversights. The anti-rationalism of science is partly justified, as a preservation of its useful methodology; it is partly mere irrational prejudice.[27]

The pattern is one Whitehead has made famous by giving it a name: The Fallacy of Misplaced Concreteness.

Conceptual attachments are part of the legacy of modern science, which emerged in a civilization with a "Greek cognitive bias."[28] In the West, many things could be left to an individual's discretion, but the question of what is to be believed was never one of these. Not until the nineteenth century, indeed, did it become possible in the West to oppose belief in God, or a heaven and hell beyond the grave, without being ostracized, jailed, exiled, or burned at the stake as one possessed by demons or addled of wit. The executions of Socrates, Savonarola, and thousands of men and women during the Spanish Inquisition constitute only the unforgettable and incredible reminders. As recently as Rousseau's *Social Contract*, "dogmas of civil religion" were mandatory for all. Refusal to accept them brought banishment from the community; falsely swearing one's belief was punishable by death. As late as 1900, America's major philosopher of science, Charles Peirce, could write the disturbing words: "Wherever you are, let it be known that you seriously hold a tabooed belief, and you may be perfectly sure of being treated with a cruelty no less brutal but more refined than hunting you like a wolf. Thus, the greatest intellectual benefactors of mankind have never dared, and dare not now, to utter the whole of their thought."[29]

Overwhelmingly today, the conceptual foundations some philosophers consider the essence of modern science are instruments for behavioral control. They are the railings of contemporary humanity's invisible stockade. As Henri Bergson declared, the brain is a reducing-valve, its conceptual productions impoverishing the affirmation of worth that is life itself. Concepts impoverish the future by directing individuals to-

27. Alfred North Whitehead, *Science and the Modern World*, p. 200.
28. The phrase is from Robert K. Bellah, *Beyond Belief*.
29. *Collected Papers of Charles Sanders Peirce*, vol. 5, par. 386.

ward outcomes determined in advance—this in a world becoming more and more unpredictable with each passing year.

Contrary to widespread opinion in the West, Buddhism's
critical attitude toward conceptual systems does not lead to
social withdrawal. One of the outstanding exponents of Pure
Land Buddhism during the Meiji Period, Manshi Kiyozawa
insists repeatedly that the condition of having "no fixed intellectual abode," or "no abiding place," is "the motto of people
active in serving the public; their activities flourish in lively
and enthusiastic fashion. They are fervent in purpose. We can
say that they are quite alive without a dwelling in a world
whose limits are known."[30]

Buddhism considers conceptual tools, logical constructs, and
postulational systems as instruments for penetrating more
deeply into new dimensions of experience. In the Buddhist
orientation, reason is also a lure or searchlight opening the
mind to wider angles of perception, deepening an ego-centered,
culture-encapsulated, dogmatic and opinionated rearing. Life
is never threatened, therefore, when the ancestral doctrine
has been cast in doubt. Significant learning occurs beneath
the conceptual level, beyond the range of linguistic systems.

It will be for the future to decide whether and how the two
self-corrective communities of the species *Homo correctus*—
Buddhism and modern science—encounter one another and
enter into relations of mutual understanding and support. If
they can collaborate in some accelerating degree, and if the
collaboration can be publicly acknowledged over the media of
the electric age, the earth will have identified the malady no
existing culture-world has been able to cure.

In a larger sense, however, the encounter is at present a
reality that remains to be more widely acknowledged. Thousands of individuals have already perceived their converging
lines, and their observations have been quoted throughout the
world. Einstein was one of these, and it is impossible to avoid
the conclusion that he felt deep kinship in both communities

30. *Selected Essays of Manshi Kiyozawa*, p. 118.

because, like himself, both belong to the living earth rather than to any finite establishment and tradition. Far from being the kind of generous conclusion that might come to mind on the centennial of Einstein's birth, there are remarks scattered through his legacy indicating how sharply he perceived the cultural encapsulation of his neighbors. Of one of the most enlightened centers of the United States, he made the following remark in a letter to his friend, Queen Elizabeth of Belgium, soon after his arrival at the Center for Advanced Studies:

Princeton is a wonderful little spot, a quaint and ceremonious village of puny demigods on stilts. Yet, by ignoring certain special conventions, I have been able to create for myself an atmosphere conducive to study and free from distraction. Here, the people who compose what is called "society" enjoy even less freedom than their counterparts in Europe. Yet they seem unaware of this restriction since their way of life tends to inhibit personality development from childhood.[31]

Thousands of individuals less famous than Einstein have felt as he. It is a conservative figure. Deep currents beneath the troubled waters of the world have been bringing large numbers of individuals to create within themselves an interface between Buddhism and modern science. Some of these remain anonymous by reason of their embeddedness in a non-Western culture, as described by Werner Heisenberg:

The great scientific contribution in theoretical physics that has come from Japan since the last war may be an indication of a certain relationship between the philosophical ideas in the tradition of the Far East and the philosophical substance of quantum theory. It may be easier to adapt oneself to the quantum-theoretical concept of reality when one has not gone through the naive materialistic way of thinking that still prevailed in Europe in the first decades of this century.[32]

The hegemony of Western civilization has come to an end, particularly over the domain of physics, where individuals are

31. Quoted in Ronald W. Clark, *Einstein*, p. 529.
32. Werner Heisenberg, *Physics and Philosophy*, p. 202.

acquiring an understanding that greatly aggravates the demands made upon intelligence and stimulates their sociological functioning beyond anything that has been known in the past. Fritjof Capra has lectured and written widely on what could be called a "counter culture" or a phrase denoting something far more surreptitious—something on the scale of the French Underground in World War II—except that these terms have been preempted by other claims upon the intellect which would serve to render ambiguous what Capra has in mind:

Mahayana Buddhists insist that the theory of interpenetration is not comprehensible intellectually but is to be experienced by an enlightened mind which transcends the dualism of logic. In modern physics, we do not have to be enlightened but are forced by nature to accept concepts which are no longer intelligible. The concept of human consciousness has been playing a central role in Eastern philosophy, and especially in Buddhism, throughout centuries, and the conclusions Buddhists have reached differ often from the ideas held in the West. If we really want to include human consciousness in our realm of research, a study of Eastern ideas might conceivably provide us with the new viewpoint which many physicists feel is very much needed in physics today. It is truly amazing that the human mind should have arrived at this organic view of an interrelated world in two so different ways.[33]

The perspective here can be broadened to include other new possibilities pressed upon us by promise being unveiled on the interface of biology, neurology, molecular biology, psychology and genetic engineering. Problems addressed in these sciences, such as the possible control and modification of the nervous system, of human potentiality and achievement, of the child's capacity for learning, and of a human-made evolution towards creatures superior to humanity as we know it, all force the forging of new relationships, new social and political systems, and a new global mode of sociological functioning. In the words of the director for scientific affairs in the Organization for European Cooperation and Development, "Science is itself becoming a kaleidoscopic, kinetic evolutionary activ-

33. Fritjof Capra, "Bootstrap and Buddhism," pp. 18–19.

ity for which present attitudes and structures are archaic; present structures of government and of learning are not geared to the new necessities."[34]

Buddhism is the world's most obvious countervailing influence to the defilements that destroy intelligence—the most obvious influence on the scale that is needed if the new global mode of sociological functioning is to prevail. Its major contribution is the method of freedom—meditation—which is capable of fostering the unfettered individual activity called for if the two self-corrective communities are to synthesize their respective capabilities in a new moment of relational power. Commencing at the outset in conferences in the Orient and the West, an existing global community might give birth to those "physicians of culture" Nietzsche considered essential if civilization is to survive. Members attending prolonged meetings of this kind might rediscover what it means to be alive, active, feeling, thinking, responding, rethinking, remembering, and enjoying in their fleeting passage the fellow-feeling-ful communication that can come as though out of the Void to correct us all. It would be an absurd and humiliating shock for a planet as richly endowed as ours to have undergone millions of years in preparing the conditions for a species whose members would struggle and win against apparently insurmountable obstacles, only to fall victim to various pathological states of madness when the awareness of the organic unity of humankind seemed about to emerge.

Both self-corrective communities serve to challenge humanity to burst its provincial cultural, intellectual, and spiritual bonds. The human world has become inextricably interlocked with itself; the separate parts are being forced to converge toward one self-corrective community. It would be a vicious regress from the indefinite complexity of being truly alive and active in the present world to seek to control this burgeoning life under the dictates of its half-knowledge and archaic cultural forms. All the mystery, uncertainty, doubt,

34. Alexander King, "The Coming Science: Kaleidoscopic, Kinetic, Evolutionary," pp. 23–24.

and unpredictability of our lives serve to awaken rational minds to the danger of oversimplifying this sudden burgeoning of life. The history of all humanity exhibits great organizations operating as conditions for progress, then as organs that stunt humanity's growth. We live today at the point where the large-scale organizations of the past have turned into the most obvious curse.

It is a strange anomaly that this world's people at both ends of their long struggle out of bestiality into ever richer adventures in civilization have had and do still have difficulty discovering how to safeguard their roots in the very creativity that prepares their way, because they first lack sufficient experience, and they later build those scaffoldings and towers that require more and more of their energy and talent in their maintenance and defense. The power of creativity moving silently through the passing moment, appropriating and synthesizing experiences into novel forms of togetherness, tends to be threatened with suffocation at whatever level of civilization an evolving humankind has attained, whether among those living without the wheel, or with those who have established their first colonies in outer space. Whether the new spirit of self-correction and free unfettered activity comes too late to save us from destroying ourselves will depend upon many variables, but one of these is the power latent in the Buddhist heritage for directing human growth out of the provincialisms of the past. The destiny of the human and the more-than-human world may well depend upon the mutual understanding and support now possible between the two self-corrective legacies together as the Yang and the Yin of the self-corrective community of tomorrow.

7

The Self-Surpassing Oneness

There is a unity in the universe, enjoying value and (by its immanence) sharing value. Take the subtle beauty of a flower in some isolated glade of a primeval forest. No animal has ever had the subtlety of experience to enjoy its full beauty. And yet this beauty is a grand fact in the universe. When we survey nature and think however flitting and superficial has been the animal enjoyment of its wonders, and when we realize how incapable the separate cells and pulsations of each flower are of enjoying the total effect—then our sense of the value of the details for the totality dawns upon our consciousness. This is the intuition of holiness, the intuition of the sacred, which is at the foundation of all religion. In every advancing civilization this sense of sacredness has found vigorous expression. It tends to retire into a recessive factor in experience, as each phase of civilization enters upon its decay.

Alfred North Whitehead
Modes of Thought

EXCEPT THROUGH THEIR own choice, there are no outsiders in the universe of life. There are only people who live as though there were. They cling to the world that has been projected for them. The things that forthwith occupy their minds, even their holiest thoughts, take hold in patterns of confinement before any awareness can dawn of what is really going on. They simply fit in and acquiesce to the pressures of habit, custom, and convention, participating from time to time in the mandatory ritual and taboo, until they are able to carry out these dehumanizing deeds with no realization whatsoever that the pure experience they enjoyed when they were very,

very small had been evacuated at some point along the line, with no ceremonial recognition of what was taking place. In school, at play, on the job, and later as man or woman of the house, everyone unwittingly succumbed to what the poet, Shelley, called "the world's slow stain," and for the simplest reason: no one had discovered a word for this confinement, much less the companion word for its elimination.

Even locked away like this, evasive and indifferent to everything but rote, men and women have a sense of existence half forgotten. It is therefore only a bit extreme to say that everyone is a participant in the interiority of a world— novel, original, spontaneous, free, and organically one—that is alive with self-initiated activity in every pore. No one can ever know when or whether even those most confined may begin to choose how they shall respond, abandoning from that moment all thoughts of "fitting in" and "going along." In the middle of a sentence the moment of the switch may come upon them, initiating a deeper identity with others, creating personally their very own series of passing nows, releasing the creativity which in its confinement everyone had overlooked.

In its more fully awakened state, life is a process of self-creation, influenced radically by the creativity of others. Each has opportunities to contribute the momentary actualities to all future life. This is to take in full seriousness the "relational origination," the "central conception of Buddhism," of chapter 3.

The only clues for this unity with everything-that-is-the-case are found where they would most reasonably be expected—in the living moment as intuited, felt, undergone— merely to think of which is to cast upon it the experience of diminution or loss. This "pure experience" is a fundamental fact prior to any discrimination between this and that, prior to any analysis of experience into subject and object, thinking and being, consciousness and its content. All particular experiences originate here, where a world is forever in the making, forever merging with something beyond.[1]

1. See Seisaku Yamamoto, "The Philosophy of Pure Experience." Yamamoto acknowledges his debt to Kitarō Nishida, *A Study of Good*. White-

With a momentum the most analytic awareness never attains, each fleeting instant intuited in the lattices of reality opens every man and woman into an ontological oneness with the self-surpassing relatedness of the organic whole. The more aware one becomes to these instants budding at the rate of perhaps fifteen or twenty per second in the human rhythm of life, the more one feels vectors of relational power rising to higher qualitative levels of life. This is what is meant by "higher states of consciousness," about which so much is being written at the present time. Increasing awareness, centered in this way, lifts an individual ever more vividly into a universe that is always One, to a Oneness that is always new, to a beauty that surpasses whatsoever enters into its wholeness (including the Oneness of an earlier awakening). Whitehead affirms that "the universe, thus disclosed, is through and through interdependent. The body pollutes the mind, the mind pollutes the body. The world is a scene of solitariness in community. The individuality of entities is just as important as their community."[2]

One becomes an outsider in the simplest and most unnatural way, by participating in life through those centers of experience that may have been "peak experiences" to others, but which have become inertly someone else's, anybody's, everybody's, rubbed clean of the radiance of the intuited instant of pure experience—original, self-active, intensely alive. This is the train of thought now emerging out of Buddhism's encounter with the contemporary world. Along this same line, Whitehead writes:

In respect to one particular new birth of one centre of experience, an actual fact is a fact of aesthetic experience. The creative process is discerned in that transition by which one occasion, already actual, enters into the birth of another instance of experienced value. There is not one simple line of transition from occasion

head is likewise central in the work, which was done in part under the direction of Charles Hartshorne, then at Emory University. "Pure experience" is the basic concept of *A Study of Good*. Professor Yamamoto is now professor of philosophy at Kyoto University and has recently published a book on Whitehead.

2. Alfred North Whitehead, *Religion in the Making*, p. 87.

to occasion, though there may be a dominant line. The whole world conspires to produce a new creation. It presents to the creative process its opportunities and its limitations.[3]

Every act leaves the world with a deeper or a fainter impress of its Self-surpassing Oneness, to be taken into account and enjoyed, or ignored and disregarded, depending upon how far the actor has awakened to what is real. Except by their own ineradicable choice, there are no impoverished people, and no way exists of assuaging their poverty and powerlessness once they have borrowed from the surrounding world the thousand confinements from which the spontaneity and freedom have flown. Each person reflecting his own pathology of cultural anaemia evacuates the intensity and vividness of the fleeting instant, turning away from the wonder of a self-surpassing response to life.

In the Buddhist orientation, the choice of those who impoverish the aesthetic richness of their lives has broader and more tragic consequences still, for in their unawakened state they magnify the suffering in themselves and the rest of life by ignoring the eminent cosmic form of the creativity Buddhists call by different names—relational origination, conditioned genesis, dependent origination. The creative advance of the universe out of a past forever perishing, which yet lives forevermore, is displaced under the distractions of daily routine. Local instances of creativity are not adequate to account for the cosmic harmony and order. Creativity is all there is, the result of fleeting instants adapting to the others, moving to synthesize what could not previously be formed. Suffering, in the Buddhist perspective, is a denial of this. In their central conception—the formula of *pratītya-samutpāda* or *paticca-samuppāda*—Buddhists seek to stress the nonsubstantiality and relativity of individual phenomena. Inada writes that "at nowhere and at no time can entities ever exist by originating out of themselves, from others, from both (self-other), or from the lack of causes."[4] Suffering, in the last resort, is the denial

3. Ibid., pp. 112–115.
4. Kenneth K. Inada, *Nāgārjuna*, p. 39.

of this. In the little patch of freedom flowing at the center of his life, each individual determines what the future becomes. Suffering is the denial of this.

Everyone and everything play a role in shaping the Self-surpassing Oneness of the world. The clues are exposed to persistent probing of those unspoken depths of experience that flow through the intuitions, perceptions, memories, and intensities of every passing now. The basic change is the becoming of events incompletely determined by the interrelatedness of things. Govinda speaks of the Self-surpassing Oneness in his latest book:

All individuals (or rather all that has an individual existence) have the whole universe as their common ground, and this universality becomes conscious in the experience of enlightenment, in which the individual awakens into his true all-embracing nature. In order to become conscious of this all-encompassing nature, we have to empty ourselves from all conceptual thought and discriminating perception. This emptiness (*śūnyatā*) is not a negative property, but a state of freedom from impediments and limitations, a state of spontaneous receptivity, in which we open ourselves to the all-inclusive reality of a higher dimension. Here we realize the *śūnyatā*, which forms the central concept of the *Prajñā-pāramitā Sūtra*. Far from being the expression of a nihilistic philosophy which denies all reality, it is the logical consequence of the *anātman* doctrine of non-substantiality. *Śūnyatā* is the emptiness of all conceptual designations and at the same time the recognition of a higher, incommensurable and indefinable reality, which can be experienced only in the state of perfect enlightenment.[5]

Śūnyatā is the eminent society in which the many—the universe viewed disjunctively—become one—the universe viewed conjunctively—in that creative advance whereby the eminent member continuously becomes the new interrelatedness of things.

It is the destiny of each entity in this living world, therefore, to live in a society endlessly surpassing a past that perishes and yet lives forevermore. As Inada has written, "*Śūn-*

5. Lama Anagarika Govinda, *Creative Meditation and Multi-Dimensional Consciousness*, pp. 10–11.

yatā is the fullness of existence. It is close to Wieman's 'concrete fullness of quality.'" And elsewhere, "*Śūnyatā* actually refers to the state of completeness or fullness of being."[6]

Participation in such a society, Govinda adds,

requires complete self-dedication and surrender of one's whole being, without reservations, without holding back anything to which the ego can cling. . . . Then everything will turn into a wonder and become a door to the great mystery of life, behind which the wealth of the whole universe is hidden, together with the Great Emptiness (*śūnyatā*) which makes this plentitude possible. This may frighten us, because it is so inconceivable to our senses and appears so abysmal to our ego-centered consciousness, bent as the latter is on maintaining its own identity.[7]

While the concept of *Śūnyatā* is implied in all Buddhist systems in a general way, it became more essential to efforts to account for the universality of the enlightenment experience. The enlightenment experience was the eminent adaptation and awakening, transforming a person's life forever, for it opens us to a Oneness everywhere taking individual emergent qualities into account, with a continuity of order to which each entity could adapt as an all-embracing community of self-surpassing life.[8] Because the enlightenment experience is not something any culture-world can confer upon its members, or

6. Kenneth K. Inada, Comments on "Creativity in the Buddhist Perspective"; idem, "The Metaphysics of Buddhist Experience and the Whiteheadian Encounter," p. 483.

7. Govinda, *Creative Meditation*, pp. 14–15. Govinda goes on to explain: "The true nature of our mind embraces all that lives. The Bodhisattva vow to free all living beings is therefore not so presumptuous as it sounds. It is an outcome of the realization that only in the state of enlightenment shall we become one with all that lives" (pp. 20–21). According to E. Obermiller, "the term *śūnyatā* is common to all the Buddhist systems in general" ("The Term *Śūnyatā* and its Different Interpretations," p. 116). Cf. Charles Hartshorne's comment regarding *śūnyatā*: "I do agree with Buddhism that there is a mysterious unity not obvious in ordinary experience. Relations to their predecessors are constitutive of events, and ordinary memory and perception do not distinctly disclose this complete summation of an event's origins. Only divine memory and perception could possess this distinctness." *Creative Synthesis and Philosophic Method*, p. 273.

8. Bergson, Peirce, Alexander, Whitehead, Montague, Hartshorne and many others have concurred on creativity in this cosmic form.

individual men and women acquire from one another, it became essential to explore the possibility that enlightenment is the supreme awakening to a cosmic source radically superior in its harmonious ordering of the totality of things. Enlightenment thus retains its unrepeatable power to release in the *Bodhisattva* the commitment to all living things, on the one condition that every description or concept of the Self-surpassing Oneness must be false to its concreteness, beauty, and interrelational power. Without this, the Oneness in the manyness loses its distinctive Buddhist stamp. Even the effort to contribute the notion of "emptiness" as a safeguard against welcoming through the back door what had been abandoned through the front introduced ambiguities and interminable, inconclusive polemics and debate. It is scarcely possible now for anyone to read the voluminous literature associated with the problem. An author of one book on the subject of emptiness, Frederick Streng, comments: "Emptiness helped to dissolve the bifurcating mental process that specifies dharma and non-dharma, eternal and 'produced', nirvāṇa and saṃsāra; the term 'emptiness' functions as mental judo."[9]

The unity-giving conjunctive order within the realm of diversity—whether designated *Śūnyatā*, Nirvana, or conditioned genesis—may best be thought of as the limitless, self-surpassing "foster-mother of all becoming" in the flow of "the undifferentiated aesthetic continuum" of life. This creative cumulative presence is there, and here, not for the specialized forms of human understanding, nor to take the position of dominance in the intellectual capital of one's categorial system. It is there primarily to be present in the secret recesses of individuals whose sufferings from delicate and lonely sensibilities are alleviated by the reminder of their ontological togetherness with other suffering creatures. The "Flower Sermon" is a constant reminder that this was the major momentum of the original assembly twenty-five hundred years ago.

The animal who uses in fantastic ways the tiny island of

9. Frederick J. Streng, personal letter, June 2, 1977. See his *Emptiness*.

conscious symbol to control behavior has an ontological problem. This problem can be carried creatively, without ever being solved, by men and women who remain positively open and openly committed to the only reality there ever is—the moment in which the flower is at an unprecedented stage of blooming, the moment where the interrelated energies of photosynthesis contribute new qualities out of the foundations of the world.

In the *Bodhisattva* this centering of life in the aesthetic foundations of the world is associated with all-embracing service to all humankind. The service has as its target the freedom of every living creature to increase the depth, range, and intensity of aesthetic richness, because this is the aim that exemplifies the eternal greatness incarnate in the passage of temporal fact.[10] The *Bodhisattva* is lured by the Self-surpassing Oneness; he intuits the way the world depends upon the Oneness. He influences the creativity of the Oneness by his vow to embrace all that lives. Intuiting the limitlessness of *śūnyatā*, where the forms of this world become immersed in the formless, and the sounds of this world echo in the soundless, the *Bodhisattva* participates with fellow-creatures, anonymously enriching the aesthetic foundations of the world. All divisions between himself and others—other creatures and things—become relations in the conditioned genesis and ontological togetherness which in its sheer "thereness" is fertile with intimations of its presence.

The individual experiencing *Śūnyatā* preserves his center of individual awareness, for to abandon that would be to abandon all; yet he experiences himself in creative union with the "whole-as-it-is (*tathatā*)," as recently characterized by Matsunaga, who goes on to say: "From such an experience the concept of one who practices actions assisting the salvation of others (*bodhisattva*) is a natural product."[11] It is this creative union that is the source of the *Bodhisattva's* compassion, his identity with all of life, including those millions in the world

10. Alfred North Whitehead, *Adventures of Ideas*, p. 41.
11. Alicia Matsunaga, *The Buddhist Philosophy of Assimilation*, p. 70.

who have fallen through the social superstructure into the brute reality of the street, abandoned to their sickness and meaningless suffering, and sustained only by the strange ability of life to continue. Sensitively aware that the spirit of each is embodied in the others, the *Bodhisattva* lives this social nature of reality and represents in this respect a higher state of consciousness than the species thus far appears to understand.

It is most appropriate in our time to understand this higher level of awareness in an evolutionary mode, and one is reminded of the remark by Richard Carrington, zoologist, anthropologist, and geographer, to the effect that the further "perfectibility of man's consciousness" may grow out of the biologically-fruitful aesthetic movement to a new parameter embracing "bigger horizons than the world of science but not at all in conflict with it." In this evolutionary movement, Carrington writes, "art and religion may provide the keys to a new level of awareness in human consciousness as the shackles of superstition fall away more and more."[12]

The suggestion that Buddhism may play a positive role in reconciling the aesthetic with the scientific interests of man, and thus foster an organic and aesthetic "metamorphosis of life," has already been encountered in chapter 3, where Richard Lannoy was quoted as anticipating that the most advanced thinking of our day will be devoted to the reconciliation of these two areas of culture. Lancelot Whyte was quoted in the same connection, suggesting that this "aesthetic metamorphosis of life" is sufficiently far advanced to participate in healing the cultural fragmentation of the contemporary world.[13]

Buddhists may bridle at the notion of evolution in connection with the "perfectibility of man's consciousness" for two reasons: first, until the term was encountered in European thought, a fully developed conception of evolution had never been produced in Buddhist philosophy, nor in Hinduism, Confucianism, or any other Eastern culture;[14] and, secondly, until

12. Richard Carrington, *A Million Years of Man*, pp. 264–265.
13. Richard Lannoy, *The Speaking Tree*, p. 79; Lancelot Law Whyte, *The Universe of Experience*, pp. 98–100.
14. Hajime Nakamura, *Parallel Developments*, p. 562.

recently the idea has never been advanced that the Buddha's Enlightenment might itself undergo an evolution, attaining a breadth and intensity unimaginable under the cultural conditions of Sarnath twenty-five centuries ago. A professor in the Tokyo area, Shinkō Saeki, is presently developing this thesis into a book, basing it on parables found in the *Aṅguttara-Nikāya*, which quote the Buddha as possibly pointing his followers in this direction. "Are there more leaves in my hand than in yonder tree?" the Buddha asked. And again, "Is there more soil, or less, in my hand than in yonder field?" According to Saeki, the Buddha's questions convey the thought that the Enlightenment would grow like the leaves in the forest and eventually attain higher and higher modes of awareness of that Self-surpassing Oneness to which the Buddha was first to awaken. The Buddha's Enlightenment was the beginning of an experience that will become more all-embracing with the passage of time. The essential experience, it is suggested, would be the same: the harmony and wholeness of aesthetic quality synthesized creatively, as the moment perishes, into a novel One, a new form of togetherness in a Self-surpassing Eminent One.

Saeki's theory of an evolving Enlightenment is one of two respects in which the Buddhist philosophical legacy may undergo creative transformation in its encounter with the superindustrial age. The second of these two issues involves an ambiguity within the central conception of Buddhism, its theory of the nonsubstantiality and relativity of all events—the concept of relational origination, or conditioned genesis, the term Jayatilleke preferred. (The ambiguity is present in modern philosophy as well—in David Hume, Bergson, Bradley, Royce, Russell and others in certain aspects of their systems.)

The Buddhist form of the ambiguity is illustrated in the most striking way by the story of Fa-tsang (643–712); summoned by the Empress Wu to explain Buddhism at court, he directed that a room be built and lined with mirrors in ceiling, walls, and floor. At the center of the room he placed an image of the Buddha. Standing with a crystal ball in his own hand, Fa-tsang, the Buddha-image, and the crystal ball were reflected in everything, and everything was reflected in the crystal ball. There was no discoverable point of origin, and no center or end.

In another account, Fa-tsang proposed an image of the universe as a multidimensional network of jewels, each containing the reflections of all the others *ad infinitum*. Each jewel represented a moment of experience, and between moments there could be no obstruction, only the mutual interpenetration and interdependence of everything that happens. As Alan Watts writes in his last book: "Pick up a blade of grass and all the worlds come with it. The whole cosmos is implicit in every member of it, and every point in it may be regarded as its center. This is the bare and basic principle of the organic view."[15] This is probably what Capra means by the term, "the Tao," on which he repeatedly relies in showing, in *The Tao of Physics*, how modern physics is converging on the ancient organic Way.

It is one of the major virtues of modern process philosophy that this ambiguity is removed. The future is open; it is the way novel forms of togetherness emerge as the past is closed. Time's "arrow" is taken seriously as the succession of fleeting events, some of which we remember, but all of which are synthesized in later moments and live forevermore. Perception is also of events that have already occurred, an interval of time separating the perception from what has been perceived. Perception is no more confined to the present than memory; both presuppose the passage of events. As Hartshorne has it, "The paradigm of realistic awareness [in the strict Buddhist sense, it should be added] is rather memory than perception, since memory more obviously seems to be what perception after all also is: awareness of the past."[16]

All of us appropriate rich qualities and stimulation from those who have died, even from those who lived long before we were born; but they are unable to receive anything from us in return. Socrates' death has taught us something about the way a man might die, but nothing in our learning affects Socrates

15. Alan Watts, *Tao*, p. 35.
16. Charles Hartshorne, *Creative Synthesis*, p. 218.

in any way. Yet again, Hartshorne confirms our point: "Our knowing Plato relates us to Plato, not Plato to us. *One-way dependence of mind upon its objects is the key to all the asymmetries, and hence also the symmetries, of reality.*"[17] The flower in its present fullness has been enriched by its earlier moments in the bud; the bud is not influenced by the mature flower, nor does the adult alter his life as a child.

In removing the ambiguity, Buddhist philosophy must accept this kind of responsibility in which symmetrical relations depend upon the asymmetrical kind. A philosophy that takes symmetrical interrelatedness of everything as ultimate stops short of complete analysis of its problems. Personal identity, as we have seen, depends upon the cumulative character of experience. The most recent moment includes those that went before. Experiences become increasingly richer embodiments of the undifferentiated aesthetic flow. Each momentary self freely creates a slightly new momentary self, the later one pregnant with possibilities no earlier moment could have known. Past states may penetrate into present ones, but never present ones into past.[18]

The Self-surpassing Oneness refers to a world that is experienced in forms of togetherness which are forever new. It refers to a world where suffering results primarily from unwillingness to center life in this synthesizing qualitative flow. Such a world is sometimes located and prized so compulsively that the quality is eroded, as the freshness falls from the first love; the vital, breath-taking colorful world no longer adds to the definiteness of reality. Losing the vision of the all-embracing Eminent One, men and women seek to enjoy their lesser goods forever. Alone, with only ruins reflected in their faces, they sense their loss and alienation from what is alive. Whether their years are few or many, when the diversity and intensity of aesthetic fullness find no answering response in the neural network, they die. They are lost from the aesthetic

17. Ibid., p. 224.
18. See Ibid., p. 192.

matrix of value, incapable of contributing to the cumulative Oneness anything except their impoverishment and defeat.

It is important that the first process philosophy in history remove this ambiguity from life's self-surpassing wonder, depositing in the experience of the contemporary world a sharp awareness of the cumulative aesthetic flow which has no limit in its power to elicit response to the wonder of being alive— no limit except those men and women impose upon themselves. To be reasonable must now mean to act in that largest matrix of life, caught up in this surpassing qualitative fullness which absorbs the intellectual component and becomes actualized and incarnate in the varied wonder and splendor of this world.[19] To be rational now is to respond to this call from the aesthetic foundations of life.

19. See John Dewey, *Art as Experience*, p. 22.

BIBLIOGRAPHY

INDEX

BIBLIOGRAPHY

BUDDHISM'S PLACE in the modern world is radically connected to that of process philosophy. The literature dealing with process philosophy, like that of the Buddhist tradition, has grown beyond anyone's ability to keep abreast. The following readings are but a sample of an outlook on life that represents a radical departure from the history of philosophy in the West. A new climate of opinion is apparently being crystallized with respect to the nature of reality. Jules Lequier spoke the germinal thought: "To be is to create." Creativity has become humanity's urgent need, more central to the continuance of civilization than the fixed forms and substances of which reality in various Western philosophies was conceived to consist.

Until the rise of process philosophy, chiefly an achievement of the present century, Buddhism was the only international alternative to the way experience had been interpreted and formulated in the West. Buddhism is the first orientation in history to suggest that ultimate reality—what is "really real"—is social in the deepest sense. Nothing is independent of its contemporaries; nothing endures in its present form forever; everything is a creative part of the organic unity of the world.

The confluence of these two traditions, each developed with only the most remote influence from the other, is shedding new light into the concreteness of experience, opening the present to new possibilities for enriching its forms of life.

Great quantities of books and journal articles are appearing in both Eastern and Western Europe, the United States, and Japan which take as their focus the writings of Alfred North Whitehead, Charles Hartshorne, Charles Sanders Peirce, William James, John Dewey, Henri Bergson, and others whose names are less often mentioned—Claude Bernard, Ernest Heinrich Haeckel, Gustav Theodor Fechner, Jules Lequier, and the Weeping Philosopher, Heraclitus, of the fifth century, B.C. International societies on process philosophy have been formed, one in Japan in 1978; one emerged from a meeting at the Katholieke Universiteit Leuven in November, 1978, with Charles Hartshorne named Honorary President. The first international symposium on Whitehead was held at Bonn in August, 1981. Thousands of doctoral dissertations have taken as their theme "Whiteheadian" philosophy, the general term in the West for thinking in the process mode. Most of Whitehead's books have been translated into the major languages of the West. Even more books of the Buddhist tradition are available in these Western tongues, including the basic Buddhist scriptures listed below.

ENGLISH TRANSLATIONS OF BUDDHIST SCRIPTURES

The Book of the Discipline (Vinaya Piṭaka). Part 1 (*Suttavibhaṅga*). Translated by I. B. Horner. London: Oxford University Press, 1949.

The Book of the Discipline. Part 2 (*Suttavibhaṅga*). Translated by I. B. Horner. London: Oxford University Press, 1957.

The Book of the Discipline. Part 3 (*Suttavibhaṅga*. Translated by I. B. Horner. London: Oxford University Press, 1957.

The Book of the Discipline. Part 4 (*Mahāvagga*). Translated by I. B. Horner. London: Luzac & Co., 1952.

The Book of the Gradual Sayings (Aṅguttara-Nikāya). Vol. 1. Translated by F. L. Woodward. London: Luzac & Co., 1952.

The Book of the Gradual Sayings. Vol. 2. Translated by F. L. Woodward. London: Luzac & Co., 1952.

The Book of the Gradual Sayings. Vol. 3. Translated by E. M. Hare. London: Luzac & Co., 1952.

The Book of the Gradual Sayings. Vol. 4. Translated by E. M. Hare. London: Luzac & Co., 1955.

The Book of the Gradual Sayings. Vol. 5. Translated by F. L. Woodward. London: Luzac & Co., 1955.

The Book of the Kindred Sayings (Saṃyutta-Nikāya). Vol. 1. Translated by C. A. F. Rhys Davids. London: Luzac & Co., 1950.

The Book of the Kindred Sayings. Vol. 2. Translated by C. A. F. Rhys Davids. London: Luzac & Co., 1953.

The Book of the Kindred Sayings. Vol. 3. Translated by F. L. Woodward. London: Luzac & Co., 1954.

The Book of the Kindred Sayings. Vol. 4. Translated by F. L. Woodward. London: Luzac & Co., 1956.

The Book of the Kindred Sayings. Vol. 5. Translated by F. L. Woodward. London: Luzac & Co., 1956.

Dialogues of the Buddha (Dīgha-Nikāya). Part 1. Translated by T. W. Rhys Davids. London: Oxford University Press, 1956.

Dialogues of the Buddha. Part 2. Translated by T. W. and C. A. F. Rhys Davids. London: Oxford University Press, 1910; London: Luzac & Co., 1959.

Dialogues of the Buddha. Part 3. Translated by T. W. and C. A. F. Rhys Davids. London: Luzac & Co., 1957.

Compendium of Philosophy (Abhidhammattha-Sangaha). Translated by Shwe Zan Aung. London: Luzac & Co., 1956.

The Middle Length Sayings (Majjhima-Nikāya). Vol. 1. Translated by I. B. Horner. London: Luzac & Co., 1954.

The Middle Length Sayings. Vol. 2. Translated by I. B. Horner. London: Luzac & Co., 1957.

The Middle Length Sayings. Vol. 3. Translated by I. B. Horner. London: Luzac & Co., 1959.

The Minor Anthologies of the Pali Canon (Khuddaka-Nikāya). Vol. 1 (*Khuddaka-pātha: The Reading of Small Passages*; and *Dhammapada: Words of the Doctrine*). Translated by C. A. F. Rhys Davids. London: Oxford University Press, 1931.

The Minor Anthologies of the Pali Canon. Vol. 2 (*Udāna: Verses of Uplift*; and *Itivuttaka: As It Was Said*). Translated by F. L. Woodward. London: Oxford University Press, 1948.

The Minor Anthologies of the Pali Canon. Vol. 3 (*Buddhavamsa: The Lineage of the Buddhas*; and *Cariyāpitaka: Collection of Ways of Conduct*). Translated by B. C. Law. London: Oxford University Press, 1938.

The Minor Anthologies of the Pali Canon. Vol. 4 (*Vimanavatthu: Stories of the Mansions*; and *Petavatthu: Stories of the Departed*). Translated by Jean Kennedy and H. S. Gehman, respectively. London: Luzac & Co., 1942.

The Questions of King Milinda. Part 1. Translated by T. W. Rhys Davids. Sacred Books of the East, vols. 35–36. Oxford: Clarendon Press, 1890–1894; reprinted New York: Dover Publications, 1963.

Woven Cadences of Early Buddhists (*Suttanipāta*). Translated by E. M. Hare. London: Oxford University Press, 1947.

WORKS CITED IN TEXT

Abe, Masao. Rev. of *Christianity and the Encounter of the World Religions*, by Paul Tillich. *Eastern Buddhist* 1 (Sept. 1965): 112–122.

Allport, Gordon. *Becoming.* New Haven: Yale University Press, 1955.

Ames, Michael E. "Religious Syncretism in Buddhist Ceylon." Ph.D. dissertation, Harvard University, 1962.

Bapat, P. V., ed. *2500 Years of Buddhism.* Rev. ed. New Delhi: Government of India, 1976.

Bellah, Robert N. *Beyond Belief.* New York: Harper & Row, 1970.

Bergson, Henri. *Creative Evolution.* Translated by A. Mitchell. New York: Henry Holt & Co., 1911.

———. *Mind-Energy.* Translated by H. Wildon Carr. New York: Henry Holt & Co., 1920.

Berry, Thomas. *Buddhism.* Twentieth Century Encyclopedia of Catholicism, vol. 145. New York: Hawthorne Books, 1967.

———. Rev. of *The Religious Life of Man.* Series edited by Frederick J. Streng. *Philosophy East and West* 24 (Apr. 1974): 239–245.

Bohm, David. "The Implicate Order: A New Order for Physics." Transcribed and edited by Dean R. Fowler. *Process Studies* 8 (Summer 1978): 77–102.

Born, Max. *Physics in My Generation.* New York: Springer-Verlag, 1969.

————. *My Life and My Views.* New York: Charles Scribner's Sons, 1968.

Bronowski, Jacob. *Science and Human Values.* New York: Harper & Bros., Torchbook, 1959.

————. *The Face of Violence: An Essay with a Play.* Cleveland: World Publishing Co., 1967.

Campbell, Joseph. *The Masks of God.* 4 vols. New York: Viking Press, 1962.

Čapek, Milič. *Philosophical Impact of Contemporary Physics.* New York: Van Nostrand & Co., 1961.

————. *Bergson and Modern Physics.* Dordrecht, Holland: D. Reidel Publishing Co., 1971.

Capra, Fritjof. *The Tao of Physics.* Berkeley: Shambhala Publications, 1975.

————. "Bootstrap and Buddhism." *American Journal of Physics* 42 (Jan. 1974): 15–19.

Carrington, Richard. *A Million Years of Man: The Story of Human Development as a Part of Nature.* New York: New American Library, 1964.

Carrol, J. B., ed. *Language, Thought, and Reality: Selected Writings of Benjamin Lee Whorf.* Cambridge, Mass.: MIT Press, 1956.

Carus, Paul. *The Gospel of Buddha.* Chicago: Open Court Publishing Co., 1894.

Clark, Ronald W. *Einstein: The Life and Times.* New York: World Publishing Co., 1971.

Cobb, John B., Jr., and Jay McDaniel. "Introduction: Conference on Mahāyāna Buddhism and Whitehead." *Philosophy East and West* 25 (Oct. 1975): 393–405.

Conze, Edward. *Buddhism: Its Essence and Development.* Oxford: Bruno Cassirer, 1951.

David-Neel, Alexandra, and Lama Yongden. *The Secret Oral Teachings in Thibetan Buddhist Sects.* Translated by H. N. M. Hardy. San Francisco: City Lights Books, 1967.

Dewey, John. *Art as Experience*. New York: G. P. Putnam's Sons, 1934.

Dumoulin, Heinrich, ed. *Buddhism in the Modern World*. New York: Macmillan Co., 1976.

Filliozat, Jean. "The Psychological Discoveries of Buddhism." *University of Ceylon Review* 13 (Apr.–July 1955): 69–82.

Findlay, J. N. *The Transcendence of the Cave*. London: George Allen & Unwin, 1967.

Fromm, Erich. *The Heart of Man*. New York: Harper & Row, 1964.

Freud, Sigmund. *New Introductory Lectures on Psychoanalysis*. New York: W. W. Norton, 1933.

Gamow, George. *Thirty Years that Shook Physics*. Garden City, N.Y.: Doubleday & Co., 1966.

Gokhale, B. G. "Aesthetic Ideas in Early Buddhism." *Journal of Indian History* 50 (1974): 231–243.

Govinda, Lama Anagarika. *Creative Meditation and Multi-Dimensional Consciousness*. Wheaton, Ill.: Theosophical Publishing House, 1976.

———. *The Psychological Attitude of Early Buddhist Philosophy*. London: Rider & Co., 1961.

Gudmunsen, Chris. *Wittgenstein and Buddhism*. New York: Barnes & Noble, 1977.

Guenther, Herbert V. *Buddhist Philosophy in Theory and Practice*. Berkeley: Shambhala Publications, 1971.

———. *Philosophy and Psychology in the Abhidharma*. Berkeley: Shambhala Publications, 1974.

———. *Tibetan Buddhism in Western Perspective*. Berkeley: Dharma Publishing Co., 1977.

———. *Tibetan Buddhism Without Mystification*. Leiden, Holland; Brill, 1966.

———. *Treasures on the Tibetan Middle Way*. Berkeley: Shambhala Publications, 1971.

Hall, Edward T. *Beyond Culture*. Garden City: Doubleday, Anchor Books, 1977.

Harris, Louis. *The Anguish of Change*. New York: W. W. Norton & Co., 1973.

Hartshorne, Charles. "Bell's Theorem and Stapp's Revised View of Space-Time." *Process Studies* 7 (Fall 1977): 183–191.

———. "The Buddhist-Whiteheadian View of the Self and the Religious Traditions." *Proceedings of the Ninth International Congress for the History of Religions*. Tokyo: Maruzen, 1960.

———. *Creative Synthesis and Philosophic Method*. LaSalle, Ill.: Open Court Publishing Co., 1970.

———. Introduction to *Philosophers of Process*, edited by Douglas Browning. New York: Random House, 1965.

———. *The Logic of Perfection*. LaSalle, Ill.: Open Court Publishing Co., 1962.

———. "Personal Identity from A to Z." *Process Studies* 2 (Fall 1972): 209–215.

———. "Whitehead's Differences from Buddhism." *Philosophy East and West* 25 (Oct. 1975): 407–413.

———. *Whitehead's Philosophy: Selected Essays 1935–1970*. Lincoln, Nebr.: University of Nebraska Press, 1972.

———. "The Structure of Givenness." *The Philosophical Forum* (1960–1961), pp. 22–39.

Heidegger, Martin. "Letter on Humanism." In *Philosophy in the Twentieth Century*, edited by William Barrett and Henry D. Aiken. Vol. 3, pp. 271–302. New York: Random House, 1962.

Heisenberg, Werner. *Across the Frontiers*. New York: Harper & Row, 1974.

———. *Physics and Beyond*. New York: Harper & Row, 1971.

———. *Physics and Philosophy: The Revolution in Modern Science*. New York: Harper & Row, 1958.

Hooykas, R. "Science and Reformation." In *The Evolution of Science*, ed. by Guy S. Metraux and Francois Crouzet. UNESCO, The

International Commission for a History of the Scientific and Cultural Development of Mankind. New York: Mentor Books, 1963.

Inada, Kenneth K. Abstract of "The Ultimate Ground of Buddhist Purification." In *Proceedings of the Eleventh International Congress of the International Association for the History of Religions*, vol. 1, p. 146. Leiden, Holland: E. J. Brill, 1968.

————. "The Metaphysics of Buddhist Experience and the Whiteheadian Encounter." *Philosophy East and West* 25 (Oct. 1975): 465–488.

————. *Nāgārjuna: A Translation of His Mūlamadhyamakakārikā with an Introductory Essay*. Tokyo: Hokuseido Press, 1970.

————. "The Ultimate Ground of Buddhist Purification." *Philosophy East and West* 18 (Jan.–Apr. 1968): 41–53.

————. "Whitehead's 'actual entity' and the Buddha's 'anatman'." *Philosophy East and West* 21 (July 1971): 303–316.

Jacobson, Nolan Pliny. *Buddhism: The Religion of Analysis*. London: George Allen & Unwin, 1966; Carbondale, Ill.: Southern Illinois University Press, Arcturus Books, 1970.

————. "Buddhism, Modernization and Science." *Philosophy East and West* 20 (Apr. 1970): 1–23.

————. "Buddhism and Whitehead on the Art of Living." *Eastern Buddhist* 8 (Oct. 1975): 7–37.

————. "Buddhism's New Encounter with the Modern World." *Kalavinka* 1, no. 4 (1976): 2–9; 1, no. 6 (1976): 4–7; 2, no. 1 (1977): 5–9.

————. "Buddhist Elements in the Coming World Civilization." *Eastern Buddhist* 5 (Fall 1972): 12–43.

————. "Creativity in the Buddhist Perspective." *Eastern Buddhist* 9 (Oct. 1976): 43–63.

————. "Oriental Influences in the Philosophy of David Hume." *Philosophy East and West* 19 (Jan. 1969): 17–39.

————. "Purification and Pollution in Buddhism." In *Buddhism and Purification: A Study of Klesa*, edited by Genjun Sasaki. Tokyo: Ministry of Education, 1974.

———. "Zen and Kierkegaard." *Philosophy East and West* 10 (Oct. 1952): 13–43.

———. "The Religion of Analysis and the Spirit of Modern Science." *World Fellowship of Buddhists: Bulletin* 6, no. 5 (1969): pp. 1–8; no. 6 (1969): pp. 8–14.

James, William. "Bergson and His Critique of Intellectualism." *A Pluralistic Universe*. New York: Longmans, Green & Co., 1909.

———. *Essays in Radical Pluralism*. New York: Longmans, Green & Co., 1912.

———. *The Varieties of Religious Experience: A Study in Human Nature*. New York: Longmans, Green & Co., 1902.

Jayatilleke, K. N. *Early Buddhist Theory of Knowledge*. London: George Allen & Unwin, 1963.

Johannson, Rune. *The Psychology of Nirvana: A Comparative Study of the Natural Goal of Buddhism and the Aims of Modern Western Psychology*. London: George Allen & Unwin, 1969.

Kashyap, Bhikkhu J. *The Abhidhamma Philosophy*. Delhi: Nalanda Pali Institute, 1954.

Keith, A. Berriedale. *Buddhist Philosophy in India and Ceylon*. London: Oxford University Press, 1923.

Kierkegaard, Søren. *The Journals of Søren Kierkegaard*. Edited and translated by Alexander Dru. New York: Oxford University Press, 1938.

King, Alexander. "The Coming Science: Kaleidoscopic, Kinetic, Evolutionary." *The Center Magazine* 6 (1973): 23–25.

Kiyozawa, Manshi. *Selected Essays of Manshi Kiyozawa*. Translated by Kunji Tajima and Floyd Shacklock. Kyoto: The Bukkyo-Bunka Society, 1936.

Koller, John M. *Oriental Philosophies*. New York: Charles Scribner's Sons, 1970.

Kraus, Elizabeth M. *The Metaphysics of Experience: A Companion to Whitehead's Process and Reality*. New York: Fordham University Press, 1979.

Kubie, Lawrence S. *Neurotic Distortions of the Creative Process*. New York: Noonday Press, 1961.

————. "Unsolved Problems of Scientific Education." *Daedalus* 94 (1965): 94–98.

Laing, R. D. *The Divided Self*. New York: Pantheon Books, 1970.

————. *Knots*. New York: Pantheon Books, 1970.

————. *The Politics of Experience*. New York: Pantheon Books, 1967.

Lannoy, Richard. *The Speaking Tree: A Study of Indian Culture and Society*. London: Oxford University Press, 1971.

Leakey, Richard and Roger Lewin. *People of the Lake: Mankind and Its Beginnings*. New York: Anchor Press, 1978.

Lowe, Victor. *Understanding Whitehead*. Baltimore: Johns Hopkins University Press, 1962.

McDermott, John J. *The Culture of Experience*. New York: New York University Press, 1976.

Macomber, W. C. *The Anatomy of Disillusion*. Evanston, Ill.: Northwestern University Press, 1967.

Magness, T. *Sammā Samādhi: The Method of Samatha-Vipassanā, Based on the Teaching of Venerable Chao Khun Mongkol-Thepmuni of Thailand*. Bangkok: n.p., n.d.

Malalasekera, Gunapala Piyasena, ed. *Encyclopedia of Buddhism*. Colombo, Sri Lanka: Government Press, 1961.

————. "Aspects of Reality Taught By Theravāda Buddhism." In *Essays in East-West Philosophy*, edited by Charles A. Moore. Honolulu: University of Hawaii Press, 1951.

Mandel, David. *Changing Art Changing Man*. New York: Horizon Press, 1967.

Margenau, Henry. *Ethics and Science*. New York: D. Van Nostrand Co., 1964.

Masson-Oursel, Paul. "Indian Techniques of Salvation." In *Spirit and Nature: Papers from the Eranos Yearbooks*, ed. Joseph Campbell. Bollingen Series, vol. 30. New York: Pantheon Books, 1954.

Matsunaga, Alicia. *The Buddhist Philosophy of Assimilation.* Tokyo: Charles E. Tuttle Co. & Sophia University, 1969.

Maxwell, Nicholas. "The Rationality of Scientific Discovery." *Philosophy of Science* 41 (Sept. 1974): 247–295.

Mayr, Ernst. "The Nature of the Darwinian Revolution." *Science* 176 (June 1972): 981–989.

Merton, Thomas. *Zen and the Birds of Appetite.* New York: New Directions, 1968.

————. "D. T. Suzuki: The Man and His Work." *Eastern Buddhist* 2 (Aug. 1967): 4–7.

Moore, Charles A., ed. *Essays in East-West Philosophy.* Honolulu: University of Hawaii Press, 1951.

————. *Philosophy East and West: The First East-West Philosopher's Conference in Honolulu.* Princeton: Princeton University Press, 1946.

————. *Philosophy and Culture East and West.* Honolulu: University of Hawaii Press, 1962.

————. *The Status of the Individual in East and West.* Honolulu: University of Hawaii Press, 1968.

Murti, T. R. V. *The Central Philosophy of Buddhism.* 2d ed. London: George Allen & Unwin, 1960.

Myrdal, Gunnar. *Asian Drama: An Inquiry into the Poverty of Nations.* 3 vols. New York: Twentieth Century Fund, 1968.

Nagel, Ernest. "The Place of Science in a Liberal Education." *Daedalus* 88 (Winter 1959): 56–74.

Nakamura, Hajime. "Interrelational Existence." *Philosophy East and West* 17 (1967): 107–112.

————. *Parallel Developments: A Comparative History of Ideas.* Tokyo: Kodansha, 1975.

————. "Unity and Diversity in Buddhism." In *The Path of the Buddha,* edited by Kenneth Morgan. New York: The Ronald Press, 1956.

————. *Ways of Thinking of Eastern Peoples: India, China, Tibet, Japan.* Honolulu: East-West Center Press, 1964.

Nanananda, Bhikkhu. *Concept and Reality in Early Buddhist Thought.* Kandy, Sri Lanka: Buddhist Publication Society, 1971.

Narada Thera. *A Manual of Abhidhamma.* Colombo, Sri Lanka: Vajirārāma, 1956.

Naranjo, Claudio. *The Healing Journey.* New York: Random House, 1973.

————. *The One Quest.* London: Wildwood House, 1974.

————, and Robert E. Ornstein. *The Psychology of Meditation.* New York: Penguin Books, 1977.

Niehoff, Arthur. "Theravāda Buddhism: A Vehicle for Technical Change." *Human Organization* 22 (1963): 108–112.

Nietzsche, Friedrich. *Human, All Too Human.* Vols. 6, 7 of *The Complete Works of Friedrich Nietzsche.* Edited by Oscar Levy. New York: Gordon Press, 1974.

————. *Thus Spake Zarathustra.* Translated by Thomas Common. New York: Modern Library, 1958.

Nishida, Kitarō. "Affective Feeling." In *Japanese Phenomenology: Philosophy as a Transcultural Approach*, edited by Yoshihiro Nitta, Eiichi Shimomissē, and Hirotaka Tatematsu. Dordrecht, Holland: D. Reidel Publishing Co., 1979.

————. *Fundamental Problems of Philosophy.* Translated by David Dilworth. Tokyo: Sophia University, 1970.

————. "The Problem of Japanese Culture." Translated by Masao Abe. In *Sources of Japanese Tradition*, edited by R. Tsunoda, W. T. de Bary, and Donald Keene. New York: Columbia University Press, 1958.

————. *A Study of Good.* Translated by V. H. Viglielmo. Tokyo: Japanese Government Printing Office, 1960.

Nishitani, Keiji. "The Awakening of Self in Buddhism." *Eastern Buddhist* 2 (Sept. 1966): 1–16.

Northrop, F. S. C. Foreword to *A Whiteheadian Aesthetic*, by D. W. Sherburne. New Haven: Yale University Press, 1961.

————. *The Meeting of East and West.* New York: Macmillan Co., 1953.

————. "Naturalistic Realism and Animate Compassion." In *The Fifth Day: Animal Rights and Human Ethics*, edited by R. K. Morris and M. W. Fox. Washington, D.C.: Acropolis Books, 1978.

Nyānaponika Mahāthera. *The Heart of Buddhist Meditation*. York Beach, Maine: Samuel Weiser, 1970.

Nyanatiloka. *Buddhist Dictionary*. Colombo, Sri Lanka: Frewin & Co., 1956.

————. *Egolessness*. Colombo, Sri Lanka: Word of the Buddha, 1957.

Obermiller, E. "The Term *Śūnyatā* and its Different Interpretations." *Journal of the Greater Indian Society* 1 (1934): 105–117.

Ornstein, Robert E. *The Mind Field*. New York: Grossman Publishers, 1976.

————, and Claudio Naranjo. *On the Psychology of Meditation*. New York: Penguin Books, 1977.

P. M. Prayudha Payutto. "Problems, Status and Duties of the Sangha in Modern Society." *Visakha Puja* (May 1968): pp. 58–73.

Pande, G. C. *Studies in the Origins of Buddhism*. Allahabad, India: University of Allahabad, 1957.

Peirce, Charles Sanders. *Collected Papers of Charles Sanders Peirce*. Vols. 1–6 edited by Charles Hartshorne and Paul Weiss. Vols. 7, 8 edited by A. W. Burke. Cambridge, Mass.: Harvard University Press, 1931–1935, 1958.

Poussin, Louis de la Vallee. *The Way to Nirvana*. Cambridge: The University Press, 1917.

Price, Jeffrey Thomas. *Language and Being in Wittgenstein's "Philosophical Investigations."* The Hague: Mouton & Co., 1973.

Price, Lucien. *Dialogues of Alfred North Whitehead*. Boston: Little, Brown & Co., 1954.

Puligandla, R. "Could There Be an Essential Unity of Religions?" *International Journal for Philosophy of Religion* 2 (Spring 1971): 14–27.

————, and K. Puhakka. "Buddhism and Revolution." *Philosophy East and West* 20 (Oct. 1970): 345–354.

————. "Nāgārjuna and Māyā." *The Middle Way: Journal of the Buddhist Society* 44 (Aug. 1974): 68–71.

Ramanan, K. Venkata. *Nāgārjuna's Philosophy: As Presented in the Mahā-Prajñāpāramitā-Sāstra.* Tokyo: Charles E. Tuttle & Co., 1966.

Rhys Davids, C. A. F. *Buddhism: Its Birth and Dispersal.* London: Thornton Butterworth, 1912.

————. Rev. of *The Central Conception of Buddhism and the Meaning of the Word 'Dharma'*, by T. I. Stcherbatsky. *Bulletin of the School of Oriental Studies* 3 (1923–1925): 346–348.

————. *To Become or Not To Become.* London: Luzac & Co., 1937.

Rhys Davids, T. W. *Early Buddhism.* London: Archibalt Constable & Co., 1908.

Rogers, Carl. *Client-Centered Therapy.* New York: Houghton Mifflin Co., 1951.

Roszak, Theodore. *Unfinished Animal: The Aquarian Frontier and the Evolution of Consciousness.* New York: Harper & Row, 1975.

Santillana, G. de. *Reflections on Men and Ideas.* Cambridge, Mass.: MIT Press, 1968.

Sarathchandra, E. R. *Buddhist Psychology of Perception.* Colombo, Sri Lanka: Ceylon University Press, 1958.

Schilpp, P. A., ed. *The Philosophy of Alfred North Whitehead.* New York: Tudor Publishing Co., 1941.

Selye, Hans. *Stress Without Distress.* New York: J. B. Lippincott Co., 1974.

Slater, Robert H. L. *Paradox and Nirvana.* New York: Columbia University Press, 1951.

Snow, C. P. *The Two Cultures and the Scientific Revolution.* New York: Cambridge University Press, 1959.

Soedjatmoko. "Cultural Motivations to Progress." In *Religion and Progress in Modern Asia*, edited by Robert Bellah. New York: Free Press, 1965.

Stapp, Henry Peirce. "Quantum Mechanics, Local Causality and

Process Philosophy." *Process Studies* 7 (Fall 1977): 173–182.

———. "S-Matrix Interpretation of Quantum Theory." *Physical Review-D* 3 (Mar. 1971): 1316–1320.

———. "Whiteheadian Approach to Quantum Theory and the Generalized Bell's Theorem." *Foundations of Physics* 9 (Feb. 1979): 1–25.

Stcherbatsky, T. I. *The Central Conception of Buddhism and the Meaning of the Word 'Dharma'*. Calcutta: Susil Gupta, 1956; Delhi: Indological Book House, 1970.

———. *The Conception of Buddhist Nirvana*. Leningrad: Publishing Office of the Academy of Sciences, USSR, 1927.

———. "The Soul Theory of the Buddhists." *Bulletin of the Academy of Sciences*, USSR, 1919.

Streng, Frederick J. *Emptiness: A Study in Religious Meaning*. Nashville, Tenn.: Abingdon Press, 1967.

———. "Metaphysics, Negative Dialectic, and the Expression of the Inexpressible." *Philosophy East and West* 25 (Oct. 1975): 429–438.

Suzuki, Daisetz Teitaro. *Zen and Japanese Culture*. Princeton: Princeton University Press, 1959.

Swenson, David. *Something About Kierkegaard*. Edited by Lillian Marvin Swenson. Minneapolis: Augsburg Publishing House, 1945.

Thittila. "The Fundamental Principles of Theravada Buddhism." In *The Path of the Buddha*, edited by Kenneth Morgan, pp. 67–112. New York: Ronald Press, 1956.

Toynbee, Arnold J. *Civilization on Trial*. New York: Oxford University Press, 1948.

Warren, Henry Clarke. *Buddhism in Translations*. Cambridge, Mass.: Harvard University Press, 1896.

Waldo, Ives. "Nāgārjuna and Analytic Philosophy." *Philosophy East and West* 25 (1975): 281–290.

Watts, Alan. *The Book: On the Taboo Against Knowing Who You Are*. London: Jonathan Cape, 1969.

———. *Tao: The Watercourse Way*. New York: Pantheon Books, 1975.

Wayman, Alex. "Who Understands the Four Alternatives of the Buddhist Texts?" *Philosophy East and West* 27 (Jan. 1977): 3–23.

Welbon, Guy Richard. *The Buddhist Nirvana and Its Western Interpreters.* Chicago: University of Chicago Press, 1968.

Wheelis, Allen. *The End of the Modern Age.* New York: Basic Books, 1975.

Whitehead, Alfred North. *Adventures of Ideas.* New York: Macmillan Co., 1933.

———. *The Function of Reason.* Boston: Beacon Press, 1958.

———. *Modes of Thought.* New York: G. P. Putnam's Sons, 1928.

———. *Process and Reality.* Edited by David Ray Griffin and Donald Sherburne. New York: Free Press, 1978.

———. *Religion in the Making.* Cleveland, Ohio: World Publishing Co., 1926.

———. *Science and Philosophy.* Paterson, N.J.: Littlefield, Adams & Co., 1964.

———. *Science and the Modern World.* New York: Macmillan Co., 1927.

Whyte, Lancelot Law. *The Universe of Experience.* New York: Harper & Row, 1974.

Wieman, Henry Nelson. *The Source of Human Good.* Chicago: University of Chicago Press, 1946.

———. "Intellectual Autobiography." Unpublished manuscript in Southern Illinois University Archives, n.d.

Wittgenstein, Ludwig. *Philosophical Investigations.* Translated by G. E. M. Anscombe. Oxford: Basil Blackwell, 1958.

Wriggins, W. Howard. *Ceylon: Dilemma of a New Nation.* Princeton: Princeton University Press, 1960.

Yamamoto, Seisaku. "The Philosophy of Pure Experience." Ph.D. dissertation, Emory University, 1961.

Yampolsky, Philip B., trans. *The Platform Sutra of the Sixth Patriarch.* New York: Columbia University Press, 1967.

Zukav, Gary. *The Dancing Wu Li Masters: An Overview of the New Physics.* New York: William Morrow & Co., 1979.

Index

Abe, Masao, 73, 170
Abhidhamma, 41
Active inattention, 58
Aesthetic matrix of life, 40, 65–83, 100–101, 113, 136, 154, 163; Northrop on, 10; Peirce on, 10–11. *See also* Feeling; *Khanavāda*; Momentariness; Present centeredness; Quality
Aesthetic sensibility, 17, 65, 68, 70, 72, 79, 100, 113, 158, 162–63
Affluent society: Buddhism a major adversary of, 21, 23
Alexander, Samuel, 62, 156
Allport, Gordon, 96
Ames, Michael, 74
Anattā (denial of bifurcating substantial self), 7, 41–51, 94–102, 105, 108. *See also* Bifurcating self; Self-centeredness; Self-encapsulation
Anguttara Nikāya, 160
Anicca (transitoriness of life), 7, 40–43, 76–80, 102–6
Anukampati (Buddhist compassion), 49. *See also Bodhisattva*; Compassion
Arahant: Theravāda ideal, 25
Archimedes, 131
Aśoka (king), 12
Asymmetrical relations: Buddhist ambiguity regarding, 42–48, 160–63
Auden, W. H., 3
Authoritarianism: Buddhist opposition to, 19, 23, 25–26, 37, 67, 137
Avijjā (ignorance), 61, 110
Awareness, 9–11, 18–21, 23, 25–26, 38–40, 56, 65, 78–79, 109–17, 137–39, 152

Bacon, Francis, 123
Bapat, P. V., 63–64
Beauty, 12–15, 18, 52, 76–79, 83, 109–10, 128–29, 151, 158–63. *See also* Aesthetic matrix of life
Bellah, Robert N., 25, 144
Bergson, Henri, 62, 69, 79, 104, 144, 156, 160
Bernal, J. D., 124
Berry, Thomas, 24, 26
Bhava (forced being), 110
Bhāvanā (cultivation of mind), 110

Bifurcating self, 95–103, 110, 137–39. *See also* Self-centeredness; Self-encapsulation
Bodhagayā, 23, 39, 110
Bodhisattva, 9, 59, 99, 157–59. *See also* Buddha, Gautama; Compassion
Bohr, Niels, 59
Born, Max, 59, 126, 130
Brain: as reducing valve, 78, 142–45
British colonial rule, 25, 134
Bronowski, Jacob, 125–26, 141
Buddha, Gautama, 8–11, 19, 21, 25, 37, 41–42; appeal to experience, 19, 110; "compassionate Buddha," 51, 114, 158; Enlightenment, 9–10, 22–23, 35–36, 39–45, 102, 105, 140, 152–53, 157–59, 160–63; silence on articulate questions, 26, 101–2, 157
Buddhism, 38, 40, 43–57, 90–95, 105, 108, 133–35; adversary of the affluent society, 21; answer to ontological emptiness and rootlessness, 50; beginning at Bodhagayā, 39; not a conceptual system, 37; influence on art of, 10–15, 66–69, 79; ontological openness, 19, 65, 77–78; pragmatic bent of, 133; questions of, 41, 65; rational integrity of, 9, 37, 54–56, 74–78, 101, 108, 144, 157–58; socio-political relevance of, 4–5, 10, 17–18, 23–25, 42, 47, 51, 53, 63, 77, 85–89, 116–17, 129–33, 134–35, 139–43, 146–49. *See also* Buddha, Gautama; Compassion; Creativity; *Dukkha*; Freedom; Meditation; Nirvana; *Pratītya-samutpāda*
Buddhist writings cited in text: *Abhidhamma*, 38, 40–41, 114; *A nguttara-Nikāya*, 160; *Dhammapada*, 39, 47; *Majjhima-Nikāya*, 40, 112; *Milindapañha (Questions of King Milinda)*, 42–43, 65, 79; *Mūlamadhyamakakārikā*, 43–44, 48–49; *Nirvana Sūtra*, 14; *The Platform Sutra of the Sixth Patriarch*, 14, 64; *Prajñā-pāramitā Sūtra*, 155
Budh (to become aware); 39. *See also* Awareness
Bühler, Karl, and Wittgenstein, 143

NOLAN PLINY JACOBSON, after a long and distinguished
teaching career, is Emeritus Professor of Philosophy and
Religion at Winthrop College in South Carolina. Professor
Jacobson holds a Ph.D. from the University of Chicago and is
widely published on Hume, Marxism, the philosophy of religion,
and Buddhism. His previous book on Buddhism, *Buddhism:
The Religion of Analysis*, is also available from Southern Illinois
University Press. Professor Jacobson, between his travels to
East Asia, presently lives in Adel, Georgia. He is at work on
a new book-length manuscript, "The Deep Heart of Japan."